The Complete Book *of* Environmental, Social and Governance ESG

The Complete Book *of* Environmental, Social and Governance ESG

Amitesh Agrahari

The Complete Book *of* Environmental, Social and Governance ESG

First Edition: 2025

Amitesh Agrahari

amiteshplastics@gmail.com

website: www.skilljetplus.in

linkedin: www.linkedin.com/in/amiteshagrahari

youtube: www.youtube.com/@amiteshagrahari_369

Listen, Learn And Action (LLA)

This book is dedicated to

My Father Late Munna lal kanhiya lal surajbali Gupta,

Who inspired me study Environmental, Social

And Governance that offer solutions to all

our modern day problems in corporate world.

ABOUT AUTHOR

Amitesh Kumar is IICA certified independent director, co-founder, author, operations head with over 20+ yrs of comprehensive experience in automobile, telecommunication & medical devices manufacturing industry, he is a seasoned executive with a robust track record of strategic leadership, operational excellence, cost savings and innovative problem-solving. His professional journey is marked by significant achievements in environmental sustainability, social responsibility, corporate governance, financial oversight, and business development.

He is co-founder of Skilljet+.in and Egizmoshop, is revolutionizing online education and e-commerce platform. He's also a bestselling author with "How to Become a Plastics Expert in Just 30 Days" and "How to Become a Rich Dad Through the Easy Way", empowering plastic professionals and students with expert insights and life success strategies.

Over 20+ yrs of experience in green field project, operations excellence, strategic planning, production management, quality management, new product development, process engineering, maintenance, scm, logistics, automation, p&l, process optimization, team training and continual improvement.

Improved operational efficiency by process optimization, problem solving, boosting productivity, reducing manpower, achieved zero defects, optimizing material movement and reducing carbon footprint.

Book Objectives

This book is designed to provide you with an in-depth understanding of Environmental, Social, and Governance (ESG) principles and practices. It will equip you with the essential skills and knowledge to integrate ESG strategies into your career or organization. As ESG practices continue to evolve, the course content will be regularly updated to reflect the latest developments and trends.

Whether you're preparing for professional certifications such as the EFFAS Certified ESG Analyst, CFA Investment Certificate, or CFI Diploma in ESG, this course will lay a strong foundation for success.

Tailored for corporate directors, executives, recent graduates, and even undergraduate students, this course offers the expertise needed to thrive in the growing field of ESG. By building your competencies in ESG, you'll be well-positioned to meet the demands of the modern workforce and make a positive impact on your organization and the broader world.

Learning Outgrowths (LO)

By the end of this book, you will have gained a wealth of knowledge, skills, and competencies, empowering you to confidently navigate the evolving world of ESG. Specifically, you will:

1. **Master the Core Principles of ESG** – Gain a deep understanding of ESG principles and learn how they apply to both business practices and societal impact.
2. **Analyze ESG Impacts on Organizational Performance** – Develop the ability to assess how ESG factors influence organizational outcomes and create value for stakeholders.
3. **Identify and Manage ESG Risks and Opportunities** – Cultivate the skills to pinpoint ESG risks and leverage opportunities, helping organizations grow sustainably and responsibly.
4. **Apply ESG Frameworks and Standards** – Learn to use established ESG frameworks and standards to evaluate and report organizational performance with confidence.
5. **Integrate Ethical Investing Principles** – Understand the importance of ethical investing and learn how to seamlessly incorporate ESG factors into investment analysis and decision-making processes.
6. **Communicate ESG Insights Effectively** – Sharpen your ability to convey complex ESG data and information clearly and persuasively to both internal and external stakeholders.
7. **Develop and Evaluate an ESG Strategy** – Gain hands-on experience in creating a tailored ESG strategy for a real-world organization, and assess its effectiveness in driving long-term value.

Each module combines engaging lectures, allowing you to apply the concepts learned in practical, real-world scenarios. The course curriculum is carefully designed to provide a holistic understanding of ESG principles, equipping you with the tools to manage ESG risks, seize opportunities, and communicate data with clarity and impact.

What You'll Learn

• **Master ESG Fundamentals** – Gain a thorough understanding of ESG principles and their transformative impact on business and society.
• **Evaluate ESG Impact** – Assess how ESG factors influence organizational success and stakeholder value.
• **Identify and Manage Risks** – Learn to pinpoint ESG risks and opportunities, and develop strategies to navigate them effectively.
• **Apply ESG Standards** – Use global ESG frameworks to measure and report organizational performance with precision.
• **Incorporate ESG into Investments** – Integrate ESG considerations seamlessly into investment analysis and decision-making.
• **Communicate ESG Insights** – Master the art of presenting ESG data to stakeholders clearly and persuasively.
• **Develop Real-World ESG Strategies** – Create and evaluate effective ESG strategies for any organization, ensuring long-term success.

Requirements & Prerequisites

• No prior knowledge required – You'll learn everything you need to know about ESG (Environmental, Social, and Governance) principles, practices, and requirements from the ground up.

Who This Book Is For

• **Aspiring ESG Professionals** – If you're eager to understand how to implement ESG in organizations, this course is your gateway to mastering these essential strategies.
• **Future ESG Consultants** – Interested in starting a new career as an ESG professional or consultant? This course will give you the knowledge and tools to excel in this rapidly growing field.

Ready to shape the future with ESG? This course is your first step!

Overview of Environmental, Social and Governance ESG

Preface – Spiritual

ESG is not a new concept—it's the ancient path to save Earth. Rooted in the Vedas and Upanishads, these timeless teachings guide us towards sustainable living, social responsibility, and ethical governance. Let's embrace this wisdom today!.

Environmental (E)

In the ancient and sacred texts of the Vedas and Upanishads, the concept of environmental sustainability is not merely a matter of human necessity, but of divine order, cosmic harmony, and reverence for all life.

The Vedas speak of *Prakriti* (nature) as the divine mother, a manifestation of the divine energy, *Shakti*, who nurtures and sustains all creation. The earth, the waters, the air, the fire, and all the elements are revered as expressions of the Supreme Being, who resides in every particle of existence. Just as the soul, *Atman*, is eternal and undying, so too is the Earth's essence sacred and boundless.

In the *Rig Veda*, the Earth is called *Bhūmi Devi*—the Earth Goddess—who nourishes all beings without expectation, offering her bounty to sustain the cosmic cycle. "*Tasya bhūmiḥ prasṛtā saṃśritā, vāyur apām aditiḥ*" (Rig Veda 1.164.13) — "The Earth, like a loving mother, provides shelter and sustenance to all her children, just as the wind and waters flow in eternal harmony." This recognition of the Earth as a sacred source of life forms the foundation of environmental sustainability.

The *Upanishads* deepen this understanding, teaching that all beings—human, plant, animal, and element—are connected through the eternal *Brahman*, the Supreme Consciousness. "*Aham Brahmasmi*" (I am Brahman) — the individual soul is one with the universe, and thus, the well-being of the world reflects the well-being of the self. Harm to the Earth is harm to the self; destruction of nature is a desecration of the divine order.

Sustainability, therefore, is a practice of aligning oneself with this cosmic order. It is *Dharma*—the path of righteousness—where one acts with compassion, moderation, and respect for all life. By taking only what is necessary, preserving the sacred resources, and living in harmony with the cycles of nature, we honor the divine and sustain the balance that holds the world together.

Thus, the wisdom of the Vedas and Upanishads teaches that true sustainability is a spiritual practice—living in unity with nature, protecting it as a reflection of the divine, and ensuring the welfare of all beings for generations to come.

Social (S)

In the timeless wisdom of the Vedas and Upanishads, social responsibility is not merely a moral obligation, but a sacred duty, rooted in the understanding of interconnectedness, harmony, and the divine order of the cosmos.

The Vedas, in their deep reverence for life, teach that all beings are interconnected through *Brahman*, the supreme consciousness that pervades all existence. "Ekam Sat Vipra Bahudha Vadanti" — "Truth is one, but the wise call it by many names" (*Rig Veda 1.164.46*). This profound realization of oneness with all beings forms the foundation of social responsibility. Just as the individual soul, *Atman*, is a reflection of the universal soul, *Paramatman*, the well-being of one is inseparable from the well-being of all.

The *Bhagavad Gita* expands on this concept through the teachings of Lord Krishna. He speaks of *Dharma*, the righteous duty, as a guiding force for life. "Nahi deha-bhajam kanchit shakti-siddhih prakurvanti" (*Bhagavad Gita 3.42*) — "The material body, though bound by senses, has the power to work and contribute to the greater good." Here, Krishna emphasizes that our actions must be in service to others, transcending selfish desires. Social responsibility, therefore, is the practice of acting in accordance with *Dharma*, serving the collective good while maintaining spiritual integrity.

In the *Upanishads*, the divine truth is often conveyed through the understanding that every individual is a part of a greater whole. "Tat Tvam Asi" — "That Thou Art" (*Chandogya Upanishad 6.8.7*). This sacred teaching reveals that by acting responsibly, we serve not only ourselves but the entire universe. True social responsibility arises from seeing the divine spark in others, recognizing that their pain and joy are interconnected with our own.

Therefore, social responsibility is a spiritual practice that calls for selfless service, compassion, and respect for all beings. It is the conscious effort to live in harmony with others, uplift the needy, and contribute to the welfare of society. Through such actions, we embody *Ahimsa* (non-violence) and *Satya* (truth), cultivating a world where the divine presence is honored in all, and the balance of the cosmos is preserved.

Governance (G)

In the sacred teachings of the Vedas and Upanishads, governance is not merely a set of rules or practices, but a reflection of divine order, ethical conduct, and the harmony that must exist between the material world and spiritual principles. It is the practice of governing with integrity, transparency, and a sense of responsibility towards all beings, recognizing that every action is connected to the greater whole.

The Vedas, in their exaltation of cosmic order (*Rta*), emphasize that governance should mirror the universal principles of balance and truth. "Satyam eva jayate" — "Truth alone triumphs" (*Mundaka Upanishad 3.1.6*). This principle of *Satya* (truth) lies at the heart of governance, urging those who hold power to be transparent in their actions, to act with integrity, and to honor their duty to both shareholders and society.

The *Bhagavad Gita* further clarifies the duties of those in positions of leadership. Lord Krishna speaks to Arjuna about the role of the wise ruler, saying, "The ruler should act in accordance with dharma, maintaining justice and righteousness, without attachment to the fruits of their actions" (*Bhagavad Gita 2.47*). This teaching underscores that true corporate governance is rooted in service to the greater good, not in the pursuit of selfish gain. It is the leader's duty to uphold the ethical values of justice, fairness, and equality, providing for the well-being of all, just as a true ruler protects his people with wisdom and compassion.

The Upanishads reveal the divine truth that all beings are interconnected through *Brahman*, the supreme consciousness. "Aham Brahmasmi" — "I am Brahman" (*Mandukya Upanishad 1.2*). This awareness of oneness calls for a governance structure where the well-being of all is prioritized, where power is not hoarded, but shared with responsibility and compassion for others.

Thus, corporate governance, as envisioned in the Vedic and Upanishadic wisdom, is a practice of ethical leadership, where actions are grounded in truth, justice, and the recognition of the interconnectedness of all beings. It is the conscious effort to govern in alignment with cosmic order, ensuring that business activities contribute to the welfare of the community and the harmony of the world.

Overview – Modern

ESG: The Future of Business—Environmental, Social, and Governance

In a rapidly changing world, businesses are expected to contribute more than just profits. The way companies operate today has far-reaching implications for the environment, society, and the economy. Enter ESG—Environmental, Social, and Governance—an essential framework that guides companies on how to balance financial goals with social responsibility, environmental stewardship, and ethical governance. ESG isn't just a buzzword—it's a comprehensive, forward-thinking approach that addresses the needs of the modern world.

What is ESG?

ESG stands for Environmental, Social, and Governance. It's a set of criteria used to evaluate how companies manage risks and opportunities related to environmental impact, social responsibility, and corporate governance. Investors, consumers, employees, and regulators are increasingly looking beyond traditional financial metrics to assess the broader effects that companies have on society. In essence, ESG provides a holistic view of a company's sustainability and ethical footprint, helping stakeholders make informed decisions.

Environmental (E) – This criterion focuses on how a company manages its environmental responsibilities. The world is facing an urgent climate crisis, and businesses are expected to minimize their negative impact on the planet. This can include initiatives such as reducing carbon emissions, minimizing waste, improving energy efficiency, and using sustainable resources. Companies that prioritize environmental protection not only reduce risks associated with climate change but also tap into growing market demand for eco-friendly products and services.

Social (S) – The social aspect of ESG pertains to how a company manages its relationships with employees, suppliers, customers, and the broader community. This includes promoting workplace diversity, ensuring fair labor practices, fostering employee well-being, and upholding human rights. Companies with strong social policies are more likely to attract top talent, retain loyal customers, and build a positive reputation. This social responsibility can also extend to supporting local communities and fostering education and health initiatives.

Governance (G) – Governance refers to the leadership and internal controls that ensure a company operates ethically and transparently. It includes factors such as executive compensation, board diversity, shareholder rights, and business ethics. Companies that excel in governance demonstrate a commitment to accountability, integrity, and transparency, reducing the risk of fraud, corruption, and other unethical practices. Strong governance fosters long-term trust with investors, employees, and customers.

The Impact of ESG

The impact of ESG practices goes beyond just improving a company's image. When companies integrate ESG principles into their strategies, they create a ripple effect that benefits the environment, society, and their bottom line.

Environmental Impact – Companies that prioritize the environment can lead efforts to combat climate change by adopting green technologies, reducing carbon footprints, and ensuring resource sustainability. For example, organizations transitioning to renewable energy sources reduce their dependency on fossil fuels, contributing to a reduction in greenhouse gas emissions. In addition to mitigating climate risks, these efforts can also lead to cost savings (e.g., energy efficiency), new business opportunities (e.g., eco-friendly products), and improved brand loyalty from environmentally-conscious consumers.

Social Impact – A company's social impact is far-reaching, affecting everyone from employees to local communities to global supply chains. By ensuring fair wages, providing a safe and inclusive working environment, and promoting diversity, businesses enhance employee satisfaction and productivity. Socially responsible businesses also contribute positively to the communities in which they operate, whether through charitable initiatives, educational programs, or supporting public health. For instance, companies that adhere to fair labor practices reduce the risk of human rights violations and benefit from stronger employee retention and engagement.

Governance Impact – Strong governance ensures that companies are well-managed and transparent. This leads to better decision-making and a reduced likelihood of scandals, legal issues, or financial crises. Good governance practices also instill investor confidence, leading to more access to capital and better stock performance. Ethical governance creates an environment of trust that fosters long-term relationships with stakeholders, ultimately contributing to sustainable growth.

Why is ESG Important?

The importance of ESG in today's business world cannot be overstated. As stakeholders become more discerning, companies that fail to embrace ESG principles risk losing market share, facing reputational damage, and potentially legal consequences. The growing emphasis on ESG reflects a shift in what it means to be a responsible company. Here are some of the key reasons why ESG is critical for modern businesses:

Investor Pressure – Investors are increasingly looking for companies that demonstrate a commitment to ESG practices. Studies show that sustainable companies, which effectively manage ESG risks, are often better positioned for long-term growth. Institutional investors, including pension funds, private equity firms, and sovereign wealth funds, are demanding more transparency in ESG reporting. As a result, companies that adhere to ESG standards may attract more investment, while those that don't could face difficulties in securing capital.

Regulatory Compliance – Governments around the world are implementing regulations to encourage or mandate ESG disclosure. The European Union, for instance, has established the Sustainable Finance Disclosure Regulation (SFDR) to promote sustainability in financial markets. In the U.S., the Securities and Exchange Commission (SEC) is considering new rules that would require companies to disclose their ESG risks.

In India, the Securities and Exchange Board of India (SEBI) oversee ESG regulatory compliance. In **2021**, SEBI introduced the **Business Responsibility and Sustainability Report (BRSR)** requirement for the top 1,000 listed companies, enhancing mandatory ESG disclosures to promote transparency and accountability in business practices. As regulations become stricter, companies must adapt to meet these legal requirements or face penalties and reputational harm.

Consumer Demand – Today's consumers are more informed and conscious about the ethical and environmental impact of the products they buy. A growing number of people are making purchasing decisions based on sustainability and social responsibility. According to recent reports, a significant percentage of consumers are willing to pay more for products and services from companies that demonstrate strong ESG commitments. Companies that embrace ESG principles are better positioned to capitalize on this demand, build customer loyalty, and gain a competitive edge in their industry.

Employee Retention – Companies that demonstrate a commitment to social and environmental causes often attract top talent, particularly among younger generations. Millennial and Gen Z workers place high importance on working for companies that align with their values. Offering diversity, equity, inclusion, and sustainability initiatives not only helps recruit top-tier employees but also boosts morale and reduces turnover.

Long-Term Sustainability – ESG practices align with long-term business goals. Environmental sustainability, in particular, can lead to cost savings, reduced risk, and new revenue streams through innovative products. Socially responsible practices foster a loyal customer base, which can drive revenue growth. Strong governance practices protect companies from unethical behaviors that could damage their reputation and bottom line.

The Future of ESG

The future of ESG looks bright, as more companies and investors recognize the importance of balancing profit with purpose. As climate change, social justice, and ethical governance continue to dominate public discourse, businesses must adapt to meet the expectations of stakeholders. ESG will evolve and become an integral part of corporate culture, decision-making, and reporting standards.

To remain competitive and resilient, companies must integrate ESG into their core strategies, not as a one-off initiative but as a long-term commitment to making a positive impact on the world.

ESG is no longer optional

It's essential for businesses aiming for long-term success in a fast-evolving global landscape. By prioritizing the environment, social responsibility, and strong governance, companies not only ensure their own sustainability but also contribute to the well-being of society and the planet. Embracing ESG principles creates value across multiple dimensions—driving profitability, reducing risks, attracting investment, and fostering loyalty from both consumers and employees. For companies looking to thrive in the future, ESG is the pathway forward, leading to a more sustainable, ethical, and prosperous world.

Module 1
Introduction to ESG

Definition of ESG

ESG stands for Environment, Social, and Governance. It is a framework used to evaluate the sustainability and ethical impact of a company or investment.

Environment (E) - The environmental aspect of ESG focuses on a company's impact on the environment. It includes factors such as climate change, greenhouse gas emissions, resource depletion, waste management, pollution, and conservation. Companies with strong environmental practices aim to minimize their negative environmental impacts and promote sustainable practices.

Social (S) - The social aspect of ESG considers a company's impact on society and stakeholders. It includes factors such as labour rights, human rights, employee welfare, diversity and inclusion, community engagement, consumer protection, and product safety. Companies with strong social practices prioritize fair and ethical treatment of their employees, suppliers, customers, and the communities in which they operate.

Governance (G) - The governance aspect of ESG focuses on the systems and structures in place to govern a company. It includes factors such as board composition, executive compensation, transparency, accountability, shareholder rights, anti-corruption measures, and adherence to legal and regulatory requirements. Companies with strong governance practices prioritize ethical decision-making, integrity, and responsible management.

ESG Framework

The ESG framework aims to evaluate a company's sustainability performance and ethical practices beyond just financial considerations.

It recognizes that a company's long-term success is intertwined with its environmental impact, treatment of stakeholders, and the quality of its governance practices.

Today, investors, asset managers, and other stakeholders increasingly consider ESG factors when making investment decisions, as they seek to align their investments with their values and promote sustainable and responsible business practices

Six Principles of ESG

The principles for ESG, also known as the guiding principles or core elements, provide a framework for integrating environmental, social, and governance considerations into business practices.

ESG Principle 1: Integration

The integration principle emphasizes the integration of environmental, social, and governance factors into the core business strategy and decision-making processes. This means considering these factors alongside financial considerations to achieve sustainable and responsible outcomes.

ESG Principle 2: Materiality

• The materiality principle involves identifying and prioritizing the most significant ESG issues that are relevant to the company's industry, operations, and stakeholders.

• It focuses on understanding which issues have the potential to affect financial performance and long-term value creation. (e.g. Waste Management is material to many manufacturing companies)

ESG Principle 3: Stakeholder Engagement

• This principle highlights the importance of engaging with stakeholders, including employees, customers, suppliers, local communities, investors, and civil society organizations.

• Stakeholder engagement helps companies understand and address their concerns, expectations, and impacts while fostering transparency and accountability.

ESG Principle 4: Risk Management

• This principle emphasizes the proactive identification, assessment, and management of environmental, social, and governance risks.

• This involves implementing measures to mitigate risks, such as climate change, regulatory non-compliance, labour disputes, reputational damage, and supply chain disruptions.

ESG Principle 5: Transparency & Disclosure

• This principle promotes transparency by encouraging companies to disclose relevant ESG information to stakeholders.

• This includes reporting on ESG performance, targets, policies, and practices through mechanisms like sustainability reports, ESG ratings, and disclosures aligned with recognized frameworks such as the Global Reporting Initiative (GRI) or the Sustainability Accounting Standards Board (SASB).

ESG Principle 6: Long-term Value Creation

• This principle recognizes the importance of sustainable, long-term value creation.

• This involves considering ESG factors as drivers of financial performance, innovation, operational efficiency, and brand reputation.

• By addressing ESG issues, companies can enhance their resilience, competitive advantage, and attractiveness to investors

The Importance of ESG in Business and Society

Reasons why ESG is significant?

1. ESG is crucial for businesses and society because it promotes responsible and sustainable practices, mitigates risks, enhances long-term value creation, and contributes to positive social and environmental outcomes.

• Embracing ESG principles aligns business interests with broader societal goals, creating a win-win situation for both businesses and the communities they operate in.

2. Risk Management and Resilience Incorporating ESG considerations helps businesses identify and manage risks related to environmental, social, and governance factors.

3. Companies can enhance their resilience and reduce potential negative impacts on their operations and reputation by proactively addressing issues like climate change, supply chain disruptions, labor practices, and regulatory compliance.

4. Long-Term Value Creation: ESG factors are closely linked to long-term value creation.

• By integrating sustainability practices, businesses can identify opportunities for innovation, operational efficiency, and cost savings.

• Embracing sustainable practices and addressing societal challenges can enhance a company's competitiveness, attract investors, and contribute to its long-term financial success.

5. Reputation and Branding: ESG performance significantly influences a company's reputation and brand image.

• Consumers, employees, investors, and other stakeholders increasingly expect businesses to operate responsibly and contribute positively to society.

• Demonstrating a commitment to ESG principles can enhance brand reputation, attract customers, and foster loyalty among stakeholders.

6. Attracting and Retaining Talent: In today's competitive job market, employees are increasingly drawn to companies that align with their values.

• Businesses that prioritize ESG factors and demonstrate a commitment to sustainability and social responsibility are more likely to attract and retain top talent.

• ESG practices contribute to a positive company culture and employee satisfaction, which can improve productivity and employee engagement.

7. Access to Capital: Investors are placing greater importance on ESG criteria when making investment decisions.

• Companies that effectively manage ESG risks and demonstrate strong performance in these areas are more likely to attract investment and secure favorable financing terms.

• Many institutional investors and asset managers now integrate ESG analysis into their investment strategies, considering environmental and social factors alongside financial performance.

8. Addressing Societal Challenges: ESG principles provide a framework for businesses to actively contribute to addressing societal challenges.

• By considering the social and environmental impacts of their operations, companies can make positive contributions to issues like climate change, social inequality, and human rights. This helps build a sustainable and inclusive society.

Describe the historical and current perspectives on ESG including global trends and their implications for organizations

The evolution of ESG can be traced back several decades:

1980-1990:

1.Focus on Ethical Investing:

• The Social Responsible Investment (SRI) movement gained momentum in the 1980s, driven by concerns about issues like apartheid in South Africa and environmental degradation.

• Investors began considering the social and environmental impact of their investments and advocated for corporate responsibility.

2. Shareholder Activism:

• Shareholders started engaging with companies through activism and proxy voting to promote change on social and environmental issues.

• This era witnessed campaigns related to divestment from specific industries and calls for better corporate governance practices.

3. Rise of Corporate Social Responsibility (CSR):

The 1990s saw the formalization of CSR as a business approach. Companies began adopting CSR policies and initiatives to address their impact on society and the environment. The idea is that businesses have broader responsibilities beyond profit maximization.

1990-2010:

1. Integration of ESG Factors.

• The focus shifted from ethical investing alone to the integration of ESG factors into investment decision-making.

• Investors recognized that ESG issues could impact long-term financial performance and started considering these factors in their analyses.

2. Frameworks and Reporting Standards

• Organizations and institutions developed frameworks and reporting standards to guide ESG reporting and disclosures.

• In 1997, The Global Reporting Initiative (GRI) was launched which provided guidelines for sustainability reporting,

• In 2000, The United Nations Global Compact was launched to encourage businesses to adopt sustainable and socially responsible policies.

2010-Present:

1.Mainstreaming of ESG

• ESG considerations become mainstream. Institutional investors began integrating ESG criteria into their investment strategies.

• The focus expanded beyond negative screening to include a positive selection of companies with strong ESG performance.

2. Regulatory and Policy Developments

• Governments and regulatory bodies worldwide introduced policies and regulations to promote ESG integration.

• These measures include mandatory ESG reporting requirements and the incorporation of ESG factors into financial regulations.

• For example, the European Union's Sustainable Finance Disclosure Regulation (SFDR). In 2021, SEBI introduced the Business Responsibility and Sustainability Report (BRSR) requirement for the top 1,000 listed companies, enhancing mandatory ESG disclosures to promote transparency and accountability in business practices.

3. Investor Demand and Market Growth

• Investor demand for ESG investments surged in the 2010s, driven by concerns about climate change, social inequality, and corporate governance failures.

• The ESG market experienced significant growth, with the emergence of dedicated ESG funds, green bonds, and impact investing.

4. Focus on Climate Change

• The urgency of addressing climate change became a central focus within the ESG framework.

• Those efforts to reduce carbon emissions, transition to renewable energy, and assess climate-related risks gained prominence.

• Initiatives such as the Task Force on Climate related Financial Disclosures (TCFD) were established to enhance climate-related financial reporting

The current perspectives on ESG and the global trends that are shaping the ESG landscape, along with their implications for organizations

1. Increased Investor Focus

• Investors worldwide are increasingly incorporating ESG factors into their investment decisions.

 • They recognize that ESG issues can have a material impact on a company's long-term financial performance and sustainability.

• As a result, organizations that prioritize ESG considerations may attract more investment capital and benefit from enhanced investor confidence.

2. Regulatory Developments

• Governments and regulatory bodies are introducing new regulations and disclosure requirements related to ESG.

• For example, the European Union has implemented the Sustainable Finance Disclosure Regulation (SFDR) and the Taxonomy Regulation, which aim to standardize ESG reporting and ensure transparency. In 2021, SEBI introduced the Business Responsibility and Sustainability Report (BRSR) requirement for the top 1,000 listed companies, enhancing mandatory ESG disclosures to promote transparency and accountability in business practices.

• Organizations need to be aware of these regulations and comply with them to avoid potential legal and reputational risks.

3. Stakeholder Expectations

• Customers, employees, and other stakeholders are increasingly demanding that organizations demonstrate their commitment to ESG principles.

• Consumers are showing a preference for sustainable and socially responsible products and services.

• Employees are seeking to work for companies that align with their values. Organizations that fail to meet these expectations may face reputational damage and may struggle to attract and retain talent and customers.

4. ESG Integration in Risk Management

• ESG factors are being recognized as key drivers of business risks and opportunities.

• Organizations need to identify and manage ESG-related risks effectively to safeguard their reputation, reduce operational risks, and ensure long-term sustainability.

• By integrating ESG considerations into risk management practices, it can help organizations proactively address potential risks and seize opportunities from transitioning to a more sustainable and responsible business model.

5. Supply Chain Resilience and Transparency

• There is a growing emphasis on responsible supply chain practices. Organizations are expected to ensure that their suppliers and business partners adhere to ESG standards.

• This includes assessing and managing environmental and social risks throughout the supply chain, ensuring fair labour practices, and promoting transparency.

• Failure to address supply chain ESG risks can lead to reputational damage and disruptions in operations.

6. ESG Reporting and Transparency

• Transparency and disclosure of ESG information are becoming crucial. Investors, regulators, and stakeholders are seeking consistent and comparable ESG data to make informed decisions.

• Organizations need to enhance their ESG reporting practices, including the use of standardized frameworks, to provide accurate and reliable information on their ESG performance.

• Improved transparency can enhance trust, attract investors, and demonstrate accountability

The key ESG frameworks and standards and their role in ESG reporting and assessment

Frameworks and standards

• The frameworks and standards play a crucial role in ESG reporting and assessment by providing organizations with a structured approach to measure and report their ESG performance.

• They help organizations identify material ESG issues, set targets, and communicate their progress to investors, stakeholders, and the public.

• Furthermore, these frameworks contribute to the comparability and transparency of ESG data, enabling investors to make more informed decisions and encouraging organizations to improve their ESG practices over time.

Global Reporting Initiative (GRI)

• GRI is one of the most widely used frameworks for ESG reporting. It provides comprehensive guidelines for organizations to report on their economic, environmental, and social impacts.

• GRI Standards offer a common language for reporting, covering a range of topics such as governance, human rights, labor practices, climate change, biodiversity, and more.

• GRI aims to enhance transparency and comparability of ESG information across organizations. Sustainability Accounting Standards Board (SASB)

• SASB focuses on industry-specific ESG reporting standards.

• It identifies the most financially material ESG issues for each industry and provides guidelines for organizations to disclose relevant ESG information.

• SASB standards help organizations communicate their ESG performance in a way that is financially meaningful to investors and stakeholders.

• TCFD, established by the Financial Stability Board (FSB), provides recommendations for voluntary climate-related financial disclosures.

• TCFD helps organizations assess and disclose their climate-related risks and opportunities, with a focus on governance, strategy, risk management, and metrics and targets.

• TCFD-aligned disclosures enable investors to understand the potential financial impact of climate-related issues on organizations.

Carbon Disclosure Project (CDP)

• CDP is a global disclosure platform that focuses on climate change, water security, and deforestation.

• It provides a standardized framework for organizations to measure and disclose their environmental impacts and risks.

• CDP data is widely used by investors, supply chain partners, and customers to assess the environmental performance of organizations.

United Nations Global Compact (UNGC)

• UNGC is a voluntary initiative that encourages organizations to align their strategies and operations with ten universally accepted principles in areas such as human rights, labor, environment, and anti-corruption.

• UNGC's reporting framework helps organizations communicate their progress and contributions to sustainable development.

Ten Components of UN Global Compact

1. Communication on Progress (COP)

2. Sustainable Development Goals (SDGs)

3. Principle-Based Reporting

4. Stakeholder Engagement

5. Goals and Targets

6. Measuring and Reporting on Progress

7. Case Studies and Best Practices

8. Challenges and Opportunities

9. Assurance and Verification

10. Integration with Financial Reporting

Business Responsibility and Sustainability Report (BRSR)

India's primary ESG regulator is the Securities and Exchange Board of India (SEBI). Initially, SEBI focused on financial market regulations, but over time, it recognized the growing importance of environmental, social, and governance (ESG) factors.

In 2012, SEBI introduced the Business Responsibility Report (BRR) for the top 100 listed companies, encouraging ESG disclosures.

In 2021, SEBI replaced the BRR with the more comprehensive Business Responsibility and Sustainability Report (BRSR), which mandates detailed ESG disclosures for the top 1,000 listed companies. This move strengthens India's commitment to transparency and sustainable business practices in line with global standards.

The Application of ESG in Business And Society

Application of ESG

• The application of ESG in business and society promotes a more sustainable, responsible, and ethical approach to economic development.

• It aims to balance financial goals with social and environmental considerations, leading to long-term value creation and a more resilient and equitable future.

Key applications:

1-Business sustainability:

• Implementing ESG practices can help businesses become more sustainable in their operations.

• This includes reducing environmental impacts, improving resource efficiency, adopting renewable energy sources, and implementing waste reduction and recycling programs.

• By doing so, companies can enhance their long-term viability, reduce costs, and mitigate risks associated with environmental regulations and resource scarcity.

2-Risk Management:

• ESG factors can be used to identify and manage risks that may affect a company's reputation, operational efficiency, and financial performance.

• By considering environmental and social risks, such as climate change, human rights violations, or supply chain disruptions, businesses can take proactive measures to mitigate these risks and build resilience.

3-Enhanced brand reputation

• Companies that prioritize ESG considerations can differentiate themselves in the market and enhance their brand reputation.

• Consumers, particularly the younger generations, are increasingly conscious of sustainability and ethical issues.

• By demonstrating a commitment to responsible business practices, companies can attract and retain customers, build trust, and strengthen their brand value.

4-Access to Capital

• ESG performance has become a significant factor for investors when making investment decisions.

• Companies with strong ESG practices may have better access to capital and can attract socially responsible investors who consider sustainability criteria alongside financial returns.

• This can lead to lower borrowing costs, increased investment opportunities, and improved long-term financial stability.

5-Attracting and retaining talent

•Employees, especially millennials and Gen Z, often seek out employers that align with their values.

• Companies that embrace ESG principles can attract and retain top talent by demonstrating a social and environmental responsibility commitment.

• This can contribute to higher employee engagement, productivity, and overall organizational success.

6-Positive societal impact

• By integrating ESG principles, businesses can contribute positively to society.

• This includes creating sustainable jobs, supporting local communities, promoting diversity and inclusion, respecting human rights, and developing innovative solutions to societal challenges.

• Businesses that actively engage in ESG practices can become agents of positive change, helping address global issues such as climate change, inequality, and social injustice

Norway: A Global Leader in Environmental, Social, and Governance Practices

Norway is often considered one of the best examples of a country successfully implementing Environmental, Social, and Governance (ESG) principles. Here's how Norway stands out in each of these areas:

1. **Environmental (E)**:

Norway excels in sustainability and environmental stewardship. The country has a robust commitment to reducing its carbon footprint and mitigating climate change. Here are some ways Norway leads in environmental aspects:

- **Renewable Energy**: Norway generates almost all of its electricity (98%) from renewable sources, primarily hydroelectric power. This positions Norway as a global leader in renewable energy.
- **Carbon Neutrality**: Norway has set ambitious climate targets, aiming to achieve carbon neutrality by 2030, significantly ahead of many other nations.
- **Sustainable Resource Management**: The country places a strong emphasis on protecting natural resources, including vast forests and fisheries, through sustainable management practices.

2. **Social (S)**:

Norway is a model of social responsibility, focusing on equality, healthcare, and worker rights:

- **Social Welfare System**: The country has one of the most comprehensive welfare systems globally, ensuring that citizens have access to healthcare, education, unemployment
- benefits, and pensions.
- **Gender Equality**: Norway is known for its high levels of gender equality, with women holding significant leadership roles in both politics and business. The government mandates gender quotas for board positions in publicly listed companies.
- **Human Rights**: Norway is a champion of human rights, with policies promoting inclusivity, indigenous rights (such as those of the Sámi people), and workers' rights.

3. **Governance (G)**:

Norway's governance structure is transparent, ethical, and focused on long-term sustainability:

- **Ethical Governance**: The country is known for its low levels of corruption and high levels of political transparency. It ranks consistently high in global governance indices.
- **Norwegian Sovereign Wealth Fund**: The Government Pension Fund Global, often called the Norwegian Sovereign Wealth Fund, is one of the largest sovereign wealth funds in the world. It is notable for its strict ESG investment criteria. The fund excludes investments in companies involved in activities such as tobacco production, weapons manufacturing, and human rights violations.
- **Corporate Transparency**: Norway enforces strict corporate governance laws, requiring transparency in reporting, board structure, and shareholder rights. This ensures that businesses are held accountable for their impact on the environment and society.

Norway is a top example for ESG because it integrates environmental sustainability, social responsibility, and ethical governance into its policies and business practices. Its progressive approach to environmental goals, social welfare, and transparency in governance sets a global standard for other nations striving to implement ESG principles effectively.

Module 2
Environmental Sustainability

The Concept of Environmental Sustainability

The Concept of Environmental Sustainability

• Environmental sustainability is a concept that revolves around maintaining the health and balance of the natural environment over the long term.

• It involves practices and strategies aimed at meeting the needs of the present generation without compromising the ability of future generations to meet their own needs.

Key aspects of environmental sustainability

1. Conservation of natural resources:

• Environmental sustainability emphasizes the responsible use and conservation of natural resources such as water, air, land, forests, minerals, and biodiversity.

• This involves practices such as reducing resource consumption, promoting efficiency, and implementing sustainable management approaches.

2. Protection of ecosystems and biodiversity:

• Environmental sustainability recognizes the importance of ecosystems and the preservation of biodiversity.

• It involves protecting and restoring natural habitats, preventing species extinction, promoting ecological balance, and ensuring the sustainable use of ecosystems for the benefit of both present and future generations.

3. Mitigation of pollution and environmental degradation:

• Environmental sustainability aims to minimize pollution and the degradation of environmental quality.

• This includes reducing emissions of pollutants, minimizing waste generation, promoting proper waste management and recycling, and implementing measures to improve air, water, and soil quality.

4. Climate change mitigation and adaptation:

• Environmental sustainability addresses the global challenge of climate change.

• It involves efforts to reduce greenhouse gas emissions, transition to low-carbon technologies, promote renewable energy sources, and adapt to the impacts of climate change.

• This includes strategies such as energy conservation, sustainable transportation, and resilience planning.

5. Sustainable development:

• Environmental sustainability is closely linked to the concept of sustainable development, which seeks to balance economic growth, social well-being, and environmental protection.

• It promotes practices that integrate environmental, social, and economic considerations into decision-making processes to ensure a harmonious and equitable development trajectory.

6. Inter-generational equity:

• Environmental sustainability recognizes the interdependence of generations and seeks to ensure equity and fairness in resource use and decision-making.

• It acknowledges that actions taken today have consequences for future generations, and thus, responsible stewardship of the environment is essential to safeguard the well-being of all

The principles of environmental sustainability and their application in business operations

5 Key Principles of Environmental Sustainability

• By applying these principles, businesses can reduce their environmental footprint, mitigate risks, enhance their brand reputation, and contribute to a more sustainable future.

• Embracing environmental sustainability not only benefits the planet but can also lead to cost savings, operational efficiency, and competitive advantage in the long run

Principle 1: Conservation of Resources

In business operations, this can be achieved through measures such as:

• Adopting energy-efficient practices and technologies, such as using LED lighting, optimizing HVAC systems, and investing in renewable energy sources.

• Implementing water conservation measures, such as installing water-efficient fixtures, recycling and reusing water where possible, and optimizing irrigation systems.

• Managing raw materials effectively by reducing waste, promoting recycling and reuse, and adopting circular economy principles that minimize resource extraction.

Principle 2: Pollution Prevention

• Implementing pollution control technologies and practices to reduce emissions of harmful substances into the air, water, and soil.

• Implementing waste management strategies, including recycling and composting programs, and minimizing the generation of hazardous materials.

• Promoting the use of environmentally friendly materials and products that have lower environmental impacts throughout their lifecycle.

Principle 3: Sustainable Supply Chain management Measure:

• Evaluating and selecting suppliers based on their environmental performance, including factors such as resource usage, waste management, and emissions.

• Collaborating with suppliers to improve sustainability practices and promote responsible sourcing of materials.

• Considering the environmental impact of transportation and logistics, aiming to minimize emissions and optimize efficiency.

Principle 4: Life Cycle Thinking:

This principle involves considering the entire life cycle of a product or service, from raw material extraction to disposal, to identify and address environmental impacts at each stage. Businesses can apply this principle by:

• Conducting life cycle assessments to evaluate the environmental impacts of products or services and identify opportunities for improvement.

• Designing products for durability, reparability, and recyclability to extend their lifespan and minimize waste generation.

• Implementing take-back or recycling programs to ensure proper disposal and recovery of products at the end of their life.

Principle 5: Environmental Management Systems

Adopting environmental management systems, such as ISO 14001, can provide a structured approach for businesses to integrate environmental sustainability into their operations. This includes:

• Setting environmental objectives and targets to guide sustainability efforts.

• Establishing monitoring and reporting mechanisms to track environmental performance.

• Conduct regular audits and assessments to identify areas for improvement.

• Engaging employees in environmental awareness and training programs to foster a culture of sustainability.

Concept of Materiality in ESG

What is the Materiality Concept in ESG?

• Materiality is a concept that defines why and how certain issues are important for a company or a business sector.

• A material issue can have a major impact on the financial, economic, reputational, and legal aspects of a company, as well as on the system of internal and external stakeholders of that company.

What is a materiality assessment?

• A materiality assessment or analysis is a process in which a company identifies the ESG issues that are most important given the operating context of a business.

• It is a method to identify the ESG risks that are most important or material to an organization or its stakeholders and their relative importance.

• It is often considered the cornerstone of a company's ESG efforts.

Why Materiality Assessment Important?

• ESG materiality assessments are necessary when organizations are working to build effective ESG strategies with stakeholder buy-in and alignment. Materiality assessments reveal factors that the strategy should focus on, giving organizations a roadmap forward. It's impossible to focus on all ESG factors at once, so prioritization is critical.

• Materiality assessment allows the organization to prioritize which ESG issues to consider in the strategy as well as include in the ESG report. It guides the target setting and helps identify the key metrics to track.

• It enables timely identification of emerging issues and opportunities; thus, helps minimize the organization's risk exposure including reputational, financial and legal risks

Two perspectives of materiality

(1) The first perspective concerns the external impacts an organization's activities have on the environment and society (also known as environmental and social materiality).

(2) The actual or potential impacts of climate change risks on the organization's business and performance (also known as financial materiality)

Materiality Assessment Matrix

A Materiality Assessment Matrix is a tool used to assess and prioritize the importance of various factors based on their impact on a business and their significance to stakeholders. It is often used in sustainability, risk management, and strategic planning to identify and prioritize the most relevant issues.

Materiality Assessment Matrix table

Material Issue	Impact on Organization (High/Medium/Low)	Importance to Stakeholders (High/Medium/Low)	Priority
Climate Change	High	High	High
Employee Health and Safety	High	Medium	High
Waste Management	Medium	High	High
Corporate Governance	High	High	High
Product Quality	High	High	High
Diversity and Inclusion	Medium	High	Medium
Supply Chain Transparency	Medium	Medium	Medium
Water Usage	Medium	Low	Low
Community Engagement	Low	High	Medium
Data Privacy	High	Medium	High

Here's a simple Materiality Assessment Matrix with the x-axis representing the importance to stakeholders and the y-axis representing the impact on the organization:

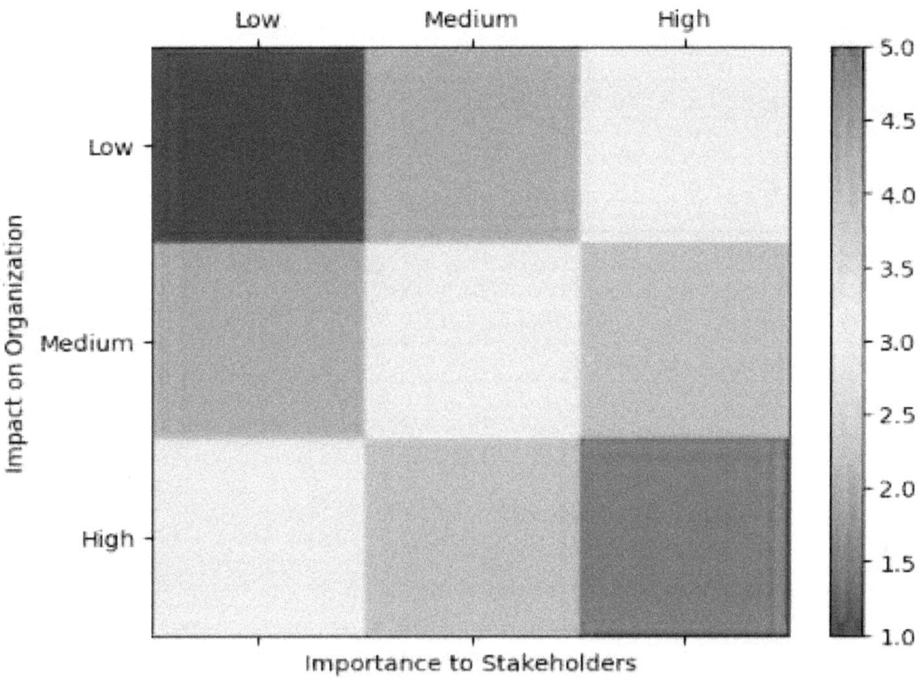

How to interpret:

- **High Impact, High Importance**: These issues should be prioritized as they are both critical for the organization and of great concern to stakeholders.
- **Medium Impact, High Importance**: Issues that are important to stakeholders but may not have an immediate, large impact on the business.
- **Low Impact, High Importance**: These are issues that are significant to stakeholders, but their impact on the organization might be lower.
- **High Impact, Low Importance**: Issues that may significantly affect the business but are not as highly regarded by stakeholders.
- **Low Impact, Low Importance**: These issues can be monitored but do not require immediate attention or significant resources.

This matrix helps organizations focus on the most relevant issues and align their strategies with both business goals and stakeholder expectations.

Example:

Impact on organization		Low	Medium	High
	Low			D
	Medium		C	
	High	B		A
		Importance to Stakeholders		

Code	Example of events
A	Termination of operating license by authority due to non-compliance on the environmental act
B	Misrepresentation of reporting
C	Community support
D	Purchase of new building to relocate

How to Conduct a Materiality Assessment?

Step 1. Build Stakeholder Assessment Team

• Assemble a team comprising internal executive leadership, management, employees, and external stakeholders to gather input on ESG factors.

Step 2. Determine Initial ESG Factors

• Collaborate with stakeholders to draft initial ESG factors, covering environmental, social, and governance aspects. Utilize established frameworks such as GRI Reporting to guide the selection of potential factors.

Step 3. Gather Feedback from Stakeholders

• Design and distribute an ESG Materiality Survey to stakeholders for rating each factor based on perceived impact, relevance, and importance.

Step 4. Synthesize Feedback to Determine Materiality

• Compile and analyze survey feedback to rank each factor. Use a materiality assessment matrix to visually represent the significance of each factor, which will be published in the final ESG reporting for disclosure. (As per the example shown in the earlier slide)

Step 5. Develop ESG Goals Based on Materiality:

• Design specific and measurable ESG goals aligned with the determined material factors as part of the overall ESG strategy efforts

Impact of climate change on the environment and its implications for organizations

Impact of Climate Change

• To navigate these challenges and opportunities, organizations need to prioritize climate resilience, adaptability, and sustainability.

This may involve implementing:

• climate risk assessments,

• incorporating climate considerations into strategic planning and decision-making,

• adopting sustainable practices,

• pursuing renewable energy sources,

• engaging in carbon footprint reduction efforts,

• investing in climate adaptation measures, and

• staying informed about evolving climate-related policies and regulations.

1. Rising temperatures and heatwaves:

• Climate change is leading to increased global temperatures and more frequent and intense heatwaves.

• This can result in heat stress for ecosystems, affecting plant and animal species, disrupting ecological balance, and leading to habitat loss.

• Organizations that rely on agriculture, forestry, or tourism sectors may face challenges due to changes in productivity, shifts in suitable growing regions, increased wildfire risks, and changes in customer behavior.

2. Changing precipitation patterns:

Climate change can alter precipitation patterns, leading to more frequent and intense rainfall events in some regions and prolonged droughts in others. This can result in increased risks of flooding, soil erosion, and water scarcity. Organizations in sectors such as agriculture, water management, infrastructure, and insurance may face challenges in adapting to these changes and managing associated risks.

3. Sea-level rise and coastal erosion:

• As global temperatures rise, glaciers and ice sheets melt, contributing to sea-level rise.

• Rising sea levels can lead to increased coastal erosion, saltwater intrusion into freshwater resources, and heightened risks of storm surges.

• Organizations located in coastal areas, including those in tourism, real estate, and transportation sectors, may face risks such as property damage, infrastructure disruption, and supply chain disruptions.

4. Changing ecosystems and biodiversity loss:

• Climate change can disrupt ecosystems and lead to shifts in species distribution and changes in biodiversity.

• Some species may struggle to adapt to changing conditions, leading to population declines or even extinctions.

• Organizations in sectors such as agriculture, fisheries, forestry, and conservation may face challenges related to shifts in productivity, loss of pollinators, and impacts on supply chains.

5. Increased frequency and intensity of extreme weather events:

• Climate change can contribute to more frequent and intense extreme weather events, such as hurricanes, cyclones, droughts, and wildfires.

• These events can cause significant damage to infrastructure, disrupt supply chains, and pose risks to employee safety.

• Organizations in sectors ranging from manufacturing and agriculture to insurance and emergency response may face increased operational and financial risks.

6. Regulatory and policy changes:

• Climate change is driving the implementation of policies and regulations aimed at mitigating its impacts.

• Organizations may face new requirements and standards related to greenhouse gas emissions, energy efficiency, water usage, waste management, and sustainability reporting.

• Failure to comply with these regulations can result in legal and reputational risks, while proactive engagement with climate-related policies can present opportunities for innovation and market differentiation.

The strategies for energy management and resource management and compliance with environmental regulations

Energy Management Strategies:

1. Conduct an energy audit:

• Start by assessing energy usage patterns, identifying areas of inefficiency, and setting energy reduction targets.

• An energy audit can help identify opportunities for improvement and prioritize actions.

2. Implement energy-efficient practices:

• Upgrade equipment and systems to energy-efficient models, optimize heating, ventilation, and air conditioning (HVAC) systems, install energy-efficient lighting, and implement energy management systems (EMS) to monitor and control energy consumption.

3. Embrace renewable energy:

Explore opportunities to incorporate renewable energy sources such as:

• solar panels,

• wind turbines, or

• geothermal systems into operations.

• Evaluate the feasibility of onsite generation or purchasing renewable energy from external sources.

4. Employee engagement and awareness

• Raise awareness among employees about energy conservation practices,

• Encourage behavioral changes,

• Establish energy-saving initiatives such as turning off lights when not in use,

• Optimizing equipment usage, and promoting the use of energy-efficient transportation options

The strategies for energy and resource management and compliance with environmental regulation

Resource Management Strategies:

1. Water conservation:

Identify opportunities to reduce water usage through water-efficient fixtures, leak detection and repair, and recycling/reuse initiatives.

• Implement water management plans to ensure responsible water use and reduce wastewater generation.

2. Waste management and recycling:

Develop comprehensive programs prioritizing waste reduction, recycling, and responsible disposal.

• Implement segregation practices, engage with recycling and waste management vendors, and promote a circular economy approach.

3. Sustainable procurement:

• Source materials and products from suppliers who demonstrate environmentally responsible practices.

• Consider factors such as material sustainability, packaging, and supply chain transparency. Encourage suppliers to adopt sustainable practices and provide incentives for sustainability improvements.

4. Life Cycle thinking:

• Consider the environmental impact of products and services throughout their life cycle.

• This includes design for sustainability, responsible sourcing of materials, and end-of-life considerations such as recycling and proper disposal

The strategies for energy and resource management and compliance with environmental regulations

Strategies for compliance with environmental regulations Strategies for compliance with environmental regulations:

1. Stay informed:

• Stay up to date with relevant environmental regulations and ensure a thorough understanding of compliance requirements.

• Monitor changes in legislation and consider joining industry associations or working with consultants to stay informed about compliance obligations.

2. Develop environmental management systems:

• Implement environmental management systems (EMS) such as ISO 14001 to establish a structured approach to environmental compliance.

• This includes setting objectives, conducting regular audits, and tracking performance against established targets.

3. Track and report:

• Implement robust monitoring and reporting mechanisms to track environmental performance, ensuring compliance with reporting requirements.

• This can involve tracking emissions, waste generation, water usage, and other relevant metrics.

4. Employee training and awareness:

• Provide training to employees to ensure awareness of environmental regulations and their responsibilities in compliance.

• Foster a culture of environmental stewardship by encouraging employees to report any non-compliance or environmental concerns

Analyze the impact of environmental sustainability on organizational performance and stakeholder value

Impacts of Environmental sustainability

• Environmental sustainability is no longer just a "nice-to-have" aspect for organizations but a strategic imperative.

• By integrating sustainability into their operations, companies can enhance their financial performance, mitigate risks, drive innovation, strengthen stakeholder relationships, and create long-term value for both the organization and its stakeholders.

1. Cost savings and operational efficiency:

• Embracing environmental sustainability can lead to cost savings and improved operational efficiency for organizations.

• By implementing energy-efficient practices, optimizing resource usage, and reducing waste generation, companies can lower their utility bills, minimize material and disposal costs, and improve overall resource productivity. This, in turn, enhances financial performance and profitability.

2. Risk mitigation:

• Environmental sustainability can help organizations mitigate risks associated with climate change, resource scarcity, and regulatory compliance.

• By identifying and addressing environmental risks, companies can reduce the likelihood of disruptions to their operations, supply chains, and reputations.

• This risk management approach improves organizational resilience and enhances stakeholder confidence.

3. Innovation and market differentiation:

• Environmental sustainability can drive innovation and foster market differentiation.

• Organizations that proactively develop sustainable products, technologies, and services can tap into new market opportunities, attract environmentally conscious customers, and gain a competitive advantage.

• Sustainability-driven innovation can lead to the development of breakthrough solutions that address environmental challenges while meeting customer demands.

4. Brand reputation and stakeholder engagement:

• Environmental sustainability is increasingly important to stakeholders, including customers, investors, employees, and communities.

• Organizations that prioritize sustainability and demonstrate environmental responsibility can build a positive brand reputation, enhance stakeholder trust, and attract and retain top talent.

• Engaging with stakeholders through sustainability initiatives and transparent reporting fosters stronger relationships and creates long-term value.

5. Regulatory compliance and market access:

• Environmental sustainability is closely linked to compliance with environmental regulations and standards.

• Organizations that proactively meet and exceed regulatory requirements can avoid penalties, legal issues, and reputational damage.

• Furthermore, many industries and markets increasingly demand sustainable practices, and organizations that align with these expectations gain access to new markets, partnerships, and business opportunities.

6. Social license to operate:

• Environmental sustainability plays a critical role in securing a social license to operate.

• By demonstrating a commitment to environmental stewardship, organizations can gain the support and acceptance of local communities, NGOs, and other stakeholders.

• This is particularly relevant in industries with significant environmental impacts, such as mining, energy, and manufacturing

Costa Rica: A Global Leader in Environmental Sustainability Practices

Costa Rica is widely regarded as one of the best examples of environmental sustainability. Here's how Costa Rica excels in this area:

1. **Renewable Energy**:

Costa Rica is a global leader in clean, renewable energy:

- **Nearly 100% Renewable Energy**: The country generates about 99% of its electricity from renewable sources, primarily hydropower, geothermal, wind, and solar energy. Costa Rica has achieved this by investing heavily in green energy infrastructure.
- **Commitment to Clean Energy**: Costa Rica has made renewable energy a cornerstone of its national development plan, emphasizing the importance of transitioning away from fossil fuels.

2. **Biodiversity Conservation**:

Costa Rica is known for its rich biodiversity and strong conservation efforts:

- **National Parks and Protected Areas**: Roughly 25% of the country's land area is designated as national parks or reserves, making it one of the most biodiverse countries on Earth. Costa Rica protects its rainforests, wetlands, and ecosystems, ensuring the conservation of its native species.
- **Ecotourism**: The country promotes ecotourism as a means of both conservation and economic development. By attracting tourists interested in nature and sustainability, Costa Rica generates income while preserving its natural resources.

3. **Reforestation and Forest Protection**:

Costa Rica has made remarkable strides in forest conservation and reforestation:

- **Forest Recovery**: In the past, Costa Rica faced widespread deforestation, but through government policies and incentives, the country has reversed this trend. Costa Rica has successfully increased its forest cover from around 21% in the 1980s to over 50% today.
- **Payment for Environmental Services Program**: Costa Rica established the Payment for Environmental Services (PES) program, which incentivizes landowners to protect forests and restore damaged ecosystems by compensating them for their environmental stewardship.

4. **Carbon Neutrality Goal**:

Costa Rica is a pioneer in setting ambitious climate targets:

- **Net-Zero by 2050**: Costa Rica has set a goal to become the first developing country to achieve carbon neutrality by 2050. The country is taking measures such as increasing its reliance on renewable energy, promoting electric vehicles, and reducing emissions from deforestation.
- **Carbon Offset Initiatives**: Costa Rica also invests in carbon offset programs that help to mitigate the impact of emissions, both domestically and globally.

5. **Sustainable Agriculture**:

Costa Rica is working to promote sustainable farming practices:

- **Organic Farming**: The country has embraced organic farming techniques, with a significant portion of its agricultural exports (like coffee and bananas) coming from sustainable, eco-friendly practices.
- **Agroforestry**: Costa Rica promotes agroforestry, where farmers integrate trees into their agricultural systems, which helps preserve biodiversity, improve soil quality, and increase water retention.

6. **Waste Management and Circular Economy**:

Costa Rica focuses on responsible waste management and recycling:

- **Recycling Programs**: The country has developed robust recycling programs, and cities like San José encourage citizens to separate waste, which is then processed for reuse or recycling.
- **Circular Economy**: Costa Rica is transitioning to a circular economy model, where the focus is on reducing waste, reusing materials, and recycling as much as possible to minimize environmental impact.

Costa Rica is a global role model for environmental sustainability, showcasing how a country can combine renewable energy, biodiversity conservation, reforestation, sustainable agriculture, and progressive climate policies to create a green, resilient future. Its commitment to becoming carbon-neutral and protecting its natural resources makes it one of the leading countries in environmental sustainability worldwide.

Module 3
Social Responsibility

Define Social Sustainability

• Social sustainability refers to the ability of a society or community to meet the needs of its present members while also fostering conditions for the well-being of future generations.

• It involves creating and maintaining equitable, just, and inclusive social systems that promote a high quality of life for all individuals.

• At its core, social sustainability emphasizes the fair distribution of resources, opportunities, and benefits among different social groups and strives to address social inequities, promote social justice, and protect human rights.

• It recognizes the interconnectedness of social, economic, and environmental factors and aims to integrate social considerations into sustainable development practices.

• Social sustainability recognizes that human well-being is interconnected with the health of the environment and the economy.

Key aspects of social sustainability

1. Equity and Social Justice:

• Social sustainability aims to eliminate disparities and promote equal rights and opportunities for all individuals, regardless of their socioeconomic background, race, gender, ethnicity, or other characteristics.

• It seeks to address systemic inequalities and promote fairness and social justice.

2. Community Well-being:

• Social sustainability focuses on enhancing the well-being and quality of life of communities.

• It involves fostering strong social connections, promoting inclusive governance and decision-making processes, ensuring access to basic services such as healthcare, education, housing, and transportation, and creating safe and vibrant public spaces.

3. Cultural Diversity and Inclusion:

• Social sustainability recognizes and values the diversity of cultures, identities, and perspectives within society.

• It promotes the inclusion and active participation of all individuals, celebrates cultural heritage, and respects the rights and autonomy of marginalized groups.

4. Health and Safety:

• Social sustainability emphasizes the promotion of physical and mental health, safety, and well-being for individuals and communities.

• It encompasses access to healthcare services, clean environments, safe living conditions, and social support systems.

5. Education and Lifelong Learning:

• Social sustainability recognizes education as a fundamental right and a catalyst for social progress.

• It emphasizes the provision of quality education, skills development, and lifelong learning opportunities to empower individuals and enable them to actively participate in society.

6. Social Cohesion and Resilience:

• Social sustainability aims to foster strong social cohesion and resilience within communities.

• It encourages collaboration, cooperation, and solidarity among individuals and groups, enabling them to address challenges collectively and build resilient communities

The principles of social responsibility and their application in business operations

• Social responsibility in business refers to the ethical and moral obligations that companies have towards society and the environment.

• It involves considering the impacts of business operations on various stakeholders, including employees, customers, communities, and the environment.

Principles of Social responsibility & its Application

• The principles of social responsibility can be applied through various strategies, such as the implementation of corporate social responsibility (CSR) programs, integrating sustainability into business strategies, conducting regular social and environmental audits, and reporting on social and environmental performance

• By adopting and implementing these principles, businesses can contribute to the overall well-being of society, build trust with stakeholders, enhance their reputation, and create long-term value for both their shareholders and the broader community

1. Stakeholder Engagement:

• Businesses should actively engage and involve their stakeholders, such as employees, customers, suppliers, local communities, and investors, in decision-making processes.

• This can be done through regular communication, feedback mechanisms, and transparency in operations.

• By considering the interests and concerns of stakeholders, businesses can make more informed decisions that benefit the broader society.

2. Ethical Conduct:

• Businesses should adhere to high ethical standards in their operations.

• This includes being honest, fair, and transparent in their dealings with stakeholders, respecting human rights, and complying with applicable laws and regulations.

• Ethical conduct also involves avoiding activities that may harm society or the environment.

3. Environmental Sustainability:

• Businesses should adopt environmentally sustainable practices to minimize their ecological footprint.

• This can include implementing energy-efficient measures, reducing waste and pollution, using renewable resources, and supporting conservation initiatives.

• By considering the long-term environmental impact of their operations, businesses can contribute to the overall well-being of the planet.

4- Employee Well-being and Fair Labor Practices:

• Businesses should prioritize the well-being and rights of their employees.

• This involves providing safe and healthy working conditions, fair wages, equal opportunities, and a supportive work environment.

• It also includes respecting workers' rights to freedom of association and collective bargaining

5. Community Development:

• Businesses should contribute to the development and well-being of the communities in which they operate.

• This can be done through initiatives such as supporting local employment, investing in community projects, engaging in philanthropic activities, and respecting the cultural values and needs of the community.

6. Responsible Marketing and Consumer Protection:

• Businesses should engage in responsible marketing practices and ensure the safety and satisfaction of their customers.

• This includes providing accurate and transparent information about products and services, avoiding deceptive advertising, and addressing customer complaints and concerns in a timely manner

The impact of diversity and inclusion on organizational performance and culture

Diversity and inclusion

• By embracing diversity and inclusion, organizations can drive innovation, enhance performance, and cultivate a positive organizational culture that benefits both employees and the overall success of the organization.

• It's important to note that diversity and inclusion efforts should go beyond surface-level representation and focus on creating an inclusive environment where all individuals feel valued, respected, and empowered to contribute their unique perspectives and talents.

Ways in which diversity and inclusion influence an organization:

1. Enhanced Innovation and Problem-Solving:

• A diverse workforce brings together individuals with different backgrounds, experiences, and perspectives.

• This diversity of thought and varied approaches to problem-solving can lead to enhanced innovation and creativity within the organization.

• When people from different backgrounds collaborate and share ideas, they can generate a wider range of solutions and identify opportunities that may have otherwise been overlooked.

2. Improved Decision-Making:

Inclusive organizations encourage open and inclusive decision-making processes that consider diverse viewpoints.

• When multiple perspectives are considered, decisions tend to be more comprehensive, well-rounded, and effective.

• Diverse teams bring different insights and challenge conventional thinking, leading to better decision outcomes and minimizing the risks of groupthink.

3. Attraction and Retention of Talent:

• Organizations that prioritize diversity and inclusion are more likely to attract and retain top talent. In today's global and interconnected world, individuals seek workplaces that value diversity, promote inclusivity, and provide equal opportunities for growth and development.

• By creating an inclusive culture, organizations can cultivate a diverse talent pool, harnessing the skills and experiences of individuals from various backgrounds.

4. Enhanced Employee Engagement and Productivity:

• When employees feel valued, respected, and included, they are more likely to be engaged and motivated in their work.

• Inclusive environments foster a sense of belonging, where employees can bring their authentic selves to the workplace. This leads to higher levels of job satisfaction, increased productivity, and improved overall performance

5. Expanded Market Reach and Customer Satisfaction:

• Organizations that embrace diversity and inclusion are better equipped to understand and meet the needs of diverse customer bases.

• By having a workforce that reflects the diversity of their customers, organizations can develop products and services that cater to a wider range of preferences, cultures, and perspectives.

• This can lead to improved customer satisfaction, increased brand loyalty, and expanded market reach.

6. Positive Organizational Culture:

• A culture of diversity and inclusion promotes respect, collaboration, and mutual understanding among employees.

• It fosters an environment where individuals feel safe to express themselves, share their ideas, and engage in constructive dialogue.

• Such a culture can lead to higher levels of trust, teamwork, and employee well-being

The strategies for promoting social sustainability, human rights, and labor practices and conducting social impact assessment and measurement

Strategies for promoting social sustainability

1. Develop and Implement Policies and Standards

• Organizations should establish clear policies and standards that outline their commitment to social sustainability, human rights, and fair labor practices.

• These policies should be integrated into all aspects of the organization's operations, including hiring and recruitment, employee well-being, supply chain management, and community engagement.

• Regularly review and update these policies to ensure they remain relevant and aligned with best practices.

2. Stakeholder Engagement

• Engage with stakeholders, including employees, local communities, customers, and civil society organizations, to understand their needs, concerns, and expectations.

• Actively involve stakeholders in decision-making processes, seek their input, and incorporate their feedback.

• This engagement helps to build trust, enhance accountability, and ensure that the organization's actions align with the values and priorities of the communities it serves

3. Supply Chain Transparency and Due Diligence:

• Promote transparency and conduct due diligence throughout the supply chain to ensure that human rights and fair labor practices are upheld.

• Implement mechanisms to assess and monitor suppliers, including audits, site visits, and third-party certifications.

• Encourage suppliers to adhere to internationally recognized standards, such as the UN Guiding Principles on Business and Human Rights, and provide support and capacity-building where necessary.

4. Employee Empowerment and Well-being

• Prioritize the well-being and rights of employees by providing fair wages, safe working conditions, and opportunities for professional development.

• Foster a culture of inclusion, diversity, and respect within the organization, where employees feel valued and empowered.

• Offer training programs on human rights, ethics, and diversity to promote awareness and understanding among employees.

5. Conduct Social Impact Assessments

• Implement social impact assessments (SIAs) to understand the potential positive and negative social impacts of organizational activities.

• SIAs involve a systematic evaluation of the social, economic, and environmental consequences of projects, policies, or programs.

• They help identify potential risks, develop mitigation strategies, and ensure that projects contribute positively to social sustainability and human rights. Social impacts are changes that occur in one or more of the following areas

• People's way of life

• Culture

• Community

• Political systems

• Environment

• Health and well-being

• Personal and property rights

• Fears and aspiration What are Social Impacts Categories?

• Social impact categories refer to the various areas or domains in which social initiatives, programs, or organizations can have a positive social impact on society.

• These social categories represent different aspects of human life and well-being that can be addressed through social interventions.

• It can be classified into five key categories.

1. Community and institutional structures

2. Population characteristics

3. Political and social resources

4. Individual and family changes

5. Community resources

6. Establish Social Impact Measurement and Reporting

• Develop robust frameworks and methodologies for measuring and reporting social impact.

• This involves identifying relevant social indicators, setting measurable targets, and regularly assessing and reporting progress.

7. Collaboration and Partnerships:

• Collaborate with external stakeholders, such as NGOs, government agencies, and academia, to leverage expertise, share best practices, and address common challenges.

• Engage in multi-stakeholder initiatives and partnerships to collectively promote social sustainability, human rights, and fair labor practices.

• These collaborations can amplify the impact of individual efforts and contribute to systemic change.

8. Continuous Improvement and Learning:

• Foster a culture of continuous improvement by regularly reviewing and evaluating social sustainability practices.

• Learn from successes and failures, adapt strategies as needed, and stay informed about emerging trends and best practices in social sustainability, human rights, and labor practices.

• Encourage knowledge-sharing and capacity-building among employees to drive ongoing improvement.

How to Measure Social Impact?

6 Steps to Measure Social Impacts

1. Define Social Impact Indicators

2. Collect Data

3. Analyse Data

4. Analyse Attribution and Counterfactual Social Impact

5. Reporting & Communication

6. Continuous Improvement

Step 1. Define Social Impact Indicators

• Defining and selecting specific social impact indicators or social impact metrics that capture the desired social outcomes and changes.

• These social impact indicators should be measurable, meaningful, and aligned with the goals and objectives of the intervention.

Example of Social Impact Indicators:

• Education: Literacy Rate

• Health: Mortality Rate

• Employment: Unemployment Rate

• Gender Equality: Gender Pay Gap

Step 2. Collect Data Gathering relevant data through various methods such as:

a) surveys

b) interviews

c) questionnaires

d) observations

e) Focus group

f) Online tracking

g) Social media monitoring

Step 3: Analyse Data

• Analyzing the collected data to understand the patterns, trends, and relationships between the intervention and the observed outcomes.

• This social impact analysis example can involve quantitative techniques (e.g., statistical analysis) and qualitative methods (e.g., thematic analysis).

a) Social Impact Analysis

b) Descriptive statistics

c) Qualitative data analysis

d) Impact evaluation framework

Step 4. Analyse Attribution and Counterfactual Social Impact

• Attribution Analysis: Assessing the extent to which the observed outcomes can be attributed to the specific intervention.

• Counterfactual social impact analysis: It involves comparing the outcomes with a plausible alternative scenario where the intervention did not occur, providing insights into the intervention's contribution to the impact.

• Social Impact Measurement Tools

a) Randomized Control Trials (RCTs)

b) Difference-in-Differences (DiD)

Randomized Control Trials (RCTs)

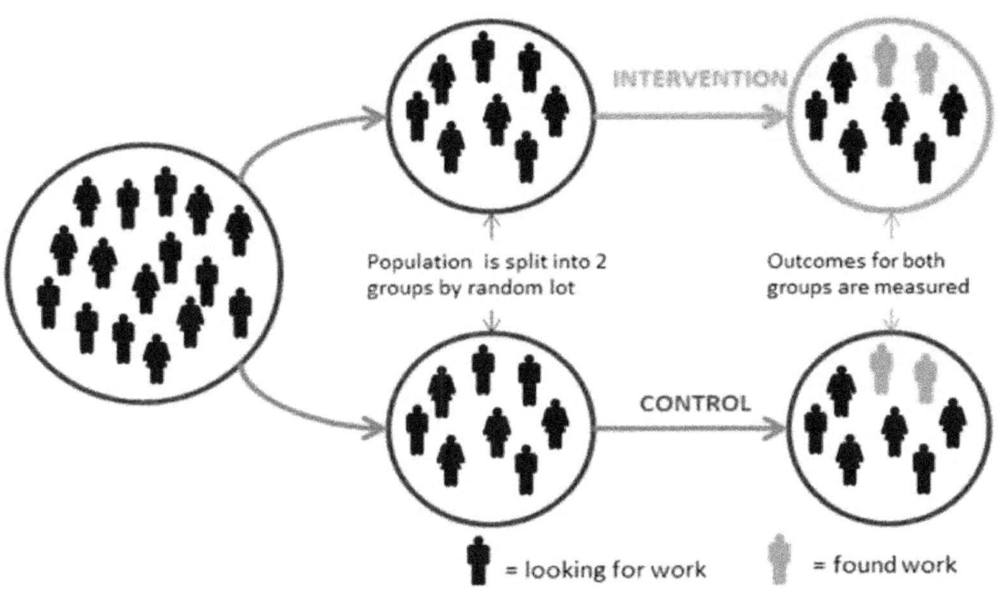

Difference-in-Differences (DiD)

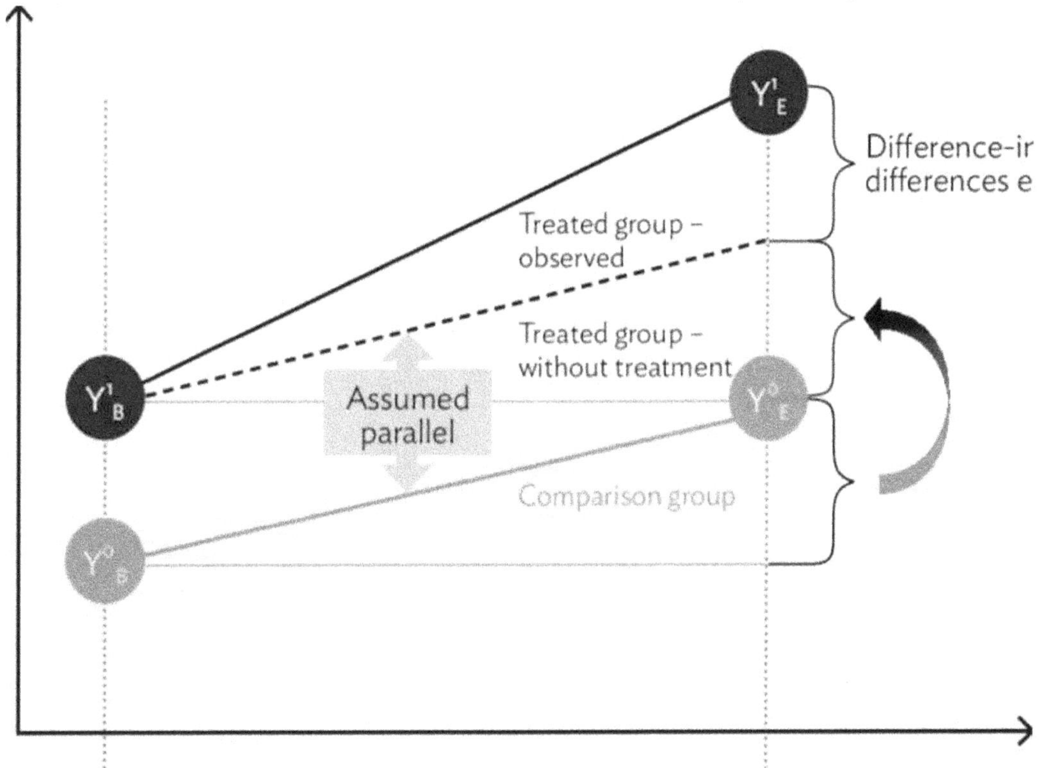

Step 5. Reporting and Communication

• Effective communication of social impact measurement results is essential for transparency, accountability, and stakeholder engagement.

• Social Impact Projects Report

a) Impact Report

b) Social Impact Study

c) Interactive Dashboards of Social Impact Projects

d) Infographics & Visualizations

Step 6. Continual Improvement

• It enables organizations to adapt their social impact strategy, interventions, and practices based on the feedback and insights gained.

• Social Impact Project Improvement:

a) Monitoring and Evaluation

b) Learning and Knowledge Sharing

c) Peer Learning Networks

Tools

Logic Model Tool: Program Action – Logic Model

Social ROI

• Use tools such as social return on investment (SROI), stakeholder surveys, and impact assessments to evaluate the effectiveness of social sustainability initiatives.

• SROI is a methodology that quantifies the social value created by an intervention or program.

• It involves assigning a monetary value to social outcomes, considering both financial and non-financial impacts, to assess the return on investment in social terms.

Tool: Social Return on Investment (SROI)

FORMULA

• SROI = SIV less IIA / IIA x 100%

Where: SIV = Social Impact Value

      IIA= Initial Investment Amount

Steps include:

(i) establishing scope and identifying key stakeholders;

(ii) mapping project outcomes with the stakeholders using the theory of change;

(iii) assigning a financial value to the project outcomes;

(iv) establishing project impact from the project end-line evaluation;

(v) calculating inputs to the project;

(vi) calculating the SROI

Tool: Theory of Change Model Tool:

The business and/or social problem we are solving is

Inputs	Processes	Outputs	Outcomes	Impact
Write all the resources you need to complete the task (people, places, funding, etc.)	What are the key activities you will conduct to reach the goal?	How will we measure the initial success of the project/initiative?	How we will see signs that the project has been effective post-initial launch?	What is the ultimate, strategic impact of the work we want to achieve? This can be bold and visionary.
Quantify the above with budgets, employee numbers, etc.	Write the key milestones and timeframes.	Short-term (0-6 months) success measurements. Example: # of people involved, % participation, etc.	Mid-term (12-18 months) success measurements. Example: follow-up survey/research results, increase sales.	Long-term (18 months onwards). Note: The impact time frame depends on the project type.

Social Impact Evaluation (SIE): 3 Steps

STEP 1: Identify impacts	STEP 2: Evaluate impacts	STEP 3: Integrate outcomes
1. Identify the stakeholders 2. Identify and describe impacts 3. Understand the social context and document the baseline 4. Document the project elements 5. Consider and document mitigations 6. Document opportunities to enhance positive impact 7. Describe the impacts after mitigation/enhancements	8. Assess likelihood and consequences of impacts occurring with the project 9. Assess likelihood and consequences of impacts occurring under the baseline 10. Assess likelihood and consequences of negative impacts after mitigations 11. Summaries the findings	12. Include impacts to be included in the economic analysis 13. Include relevant elements in reference project and other analyses 14. Include relevant elements in the appraisal summary table **15.** Update the evaluation and the risk and benefits registers

Denmark: A Global Leader in Social Responsibility and Welfare

Denmark is often considered one of the best examples of a country demonstrating social responsibility. Here's how Denmark excels in this area:

1. Welfare System:

Denmark has one of the world's most comprehensive welfare systems, ensuring that all citizens have access to essential services:

- **Universal Healthcare**: Every resident is provided with free or highly subsidized healthcare, ensuring no one is left behind due to financial constraints.
- **Education**: The country offers free public education from primary school through university, providing equal opportunities for all citizens.
- **Unemployment Benefits**: Denmark has a strong social safety net, providing financial support for unemployed individuals while they search for new job opportunities.

2. Labor Rights and Fair Working Conditions:

Denmark is known for its fair labor practices and high standards for worker rights:

- **Strong Labor Unions**: Denmark has a tradition of strong labor unions that advocate for fair wages, safe working conditions, and good benefits.
- **Work-Life Balance**: The country places a high value on work-life balance, with policies ensuring that employees are not overburdened and can enjoy time with their families.
- **Employee Rights**: Danish workers enjoy high levels of protection, including maternity and paternity leave, vacation time, and a strong legal framework for workplace safety.

3. Gender Equality:

Denmark has made significant strides in gender equality, both in the workplace and in society:

- **Equal Pay**: Denmark enforces policies to reduce the gender pay gap, and the country is often ranked highly in terms of gender equality in leadership roles.
- **Women in Leadership**: Denmark has achieved a high level of female participation in politics, with women holding positions in government and business leadership.
- **Parental Leave**: The country offers generous parental leave policies that promote equal responsibility for raising children.

4. **Sustainability and Environmental Responsibility**:

Denmark is also a leader in sustainability, which contributes to its broader social responsibility efforts:

- **Green Energy**: The country invests heavily in renewable energy, aiming to be carbon-neutral by 2050, which not only helps the planet but also improves the quality of life for its citizens.
- **Sustainable Urban Planning**: Copenhagen, Denmark's capital, is known for its bicycle-friendly infrastructure, green spaces, and efforts to reduce pollution, which fosters a high quality of life for residents.

5. **Social Inclusivity**:

Denmark is known for its inclusive policies that protect marginalized groups:

- **Immigration and Integration**: Denmark has a strong focus on the integration of immigrants, providing programs for language education, job training, and cultural inclusion.
- **Support for Vulnerable Groups**: The country provides extensive support to vulnerable populations, including the elderly, disabled individuals, and low-income families, ensuring that everyone has access to basic needs and services.

Denmark stands out as a global leader in social responsibility due to its strong welfare system, labor protections, gender equality, environmental sustainability, and inclusivity. The country's holistic approach to ensuring the well-being of all its citizens serves as a model for other nations aiming to implement social responsibility at a national level.

Module 4
Corporate Governance

Define Corporate Governance

Definition of Corporate Governance

• Corporate governance refers to the system of rules, practices, and processes by which a company is directed and controlled.

• It involves the relationships between a company's management, its board of directors, its shareholders, and other stakeholders.

• The primary objective of corporate governance is to ensure that the company operates in an accountable, transparent, and responsible manner.

Governance Factors

• Governance factors look at the structure of the board, leadership, and policies of a company.

• This includes aspects like board independence, executive compensation, shareholder rights, transparency, and business ethics.

The principles of corporate governance and their application in organization

Common Governance Principles and Applications

1. Board Independence

• The board of directors should be composed of independent non-executive directors who are not involved in day-to-day operations and are free from conflicts of interest.

• Independent non-executive directors bring objectivity, and diverse perspectives, and serve as a check on management. They ensure the board acts in the best interest of the company and its stakeholders.

2. Board Diversity and Inclusion

• Organizations should strive for diversity and inclusion within the board of directors and senior management.

• This includes diversity in terms of gender, ethnicity, age, expertise, and background.

• A diverse board brings a wider range of perspectives, fosters innovation, and better reflects the diverse interests of stakeholders.

3. Remuneration and Incentive Structures

• Organizations should establish remuneration and incentive structures that align with long-term value creation and promote sustainable performance.

• This includes considering financial and non-financial performance metrics, avoiding excessive risk-taking, and linking executive compensation to the achievement of strategic objectives and ESG goals.

4. Board Effectiveness

• The board of directors should be effective in fulfilling its responsibilities.

• This involves having a diverse mix of skills, expertise, and experience among board members.

• The board should conduct regular evaluations of its own performance and ensure its composition aligns with the strategic needs of the organization.

5. Sub-Board Committees

• The board of directors should have a robust system for overseeing and managing risks.

• This includes establishing an audit committee, risk management committee, nomination committee, and remuneration committee to ensure the leadership of the organization is effective.

6-Accountability and Responsibility

• Organizations should establish clear lines of accountability throughout the company.

• This involves defining roles and responsibilities, ensuring appropriate delegation of authority, and holding individuals and teams accountable for their actions.

• Clear accountability enhances decision-making and promotes ethical behavior.

7. Transparency and Disclosure

• Organizations should maintain transparency in their operations and disclose relevant information to stakeholders.

• This includes financial statements, governance structures, executive compensation, and ESG-related practices.

• Transparent disclosure builds trust and allows stakeholders to make informed decisions.

8. Fairness and Equity

• Organizations should treat all stakeholders fairly and equitably.

• This includes providing equal opportunities, avoiding discrimination, and respecting the rights of employees, customers, shareholders, and other stakeholders.

• Fairness and equity foster a positive organizational culture and promote long-term relationships.

9. Ethical Conduct

• Organizations should promote ethical conduct and integrity at all levels.

• This includes establishing a code of ethics, implementing robust ethics training programs, and encouraging a culture of integrity.

• Ethical conduct builds trust, enhances reputation, and mitigates risks associated with unethical behavior.

10. Risk Management Process

• Organizations should establish effective risk management processes to identify, assess, and manage risks.

• This involves adopting risk management frameworks, conducting regular risk assessments, and implementing appropriate controls and mitigation strategies.

• Effective risk management ensures the long-term viability and sustainability of the organization.

11. Shareholder Rights

• Organizations should protect and facilitate the exercise of shareholders' rights.

• This includes providing shareholders with the ability to vote on significant matters, access information, and participate in decision-making processes.

• Respecting shareholder rights enhances corporate accountability and encourages long-term investment.

12. Stakeholder Engagement

• Organizations should engage with and consider the interests of various stakeholders, including employees, customers, suppliers, communities, and the environment.

• This involves establishing mechanisms for stakeholder feedback, considering their perspectives in decision-making, and integrating their concerns into the company's strategy and operations.

13. Long-Term Value Creation

• Corporate governance should focus on creating sustainable long-term value for the organization and its stakeholders, rather than solely pursuing short-term financial gains.

• This involves aligning incentives and performance metrics with long-term objectives, considering ESG factors in decision-making, and balancing the interests of different stakeholders.

The effectiveness of board structures according to corporate governance practices

Effectiveness of board structures depends on key factors:

1. Board Composition:

• An effective board structure begins with the composition of the board of directors. It should consist of individuals with diverse backgrounds, skills, expertise, and experiences that align with the organization's strategic objectives.

• Board members should possess a mix of industry knowledge, financial acumen, legal expertise, and other relevant qualifications to provide valuable insights and guidance.

2. Independence:

• Independence is a critical aspect of an effective board structure.

• Independent directors should form a significant portion of the board, ensuring they can provide objective judgment and act in the best interests of the organization and its stakeholders.

• Independence helps maintain a system of checks and balances, reduces conflicts of interest, and enhances the credibility of board decisions.

3. Board Size:

• The size of the board should be appropriate for the organization, taking into consideration its complexity, nature of operations, and industry standards.

• While there is no universally ideal board size, it is generally recommended to strike a balance between having a sufficient number of directors to represent diverse perspectives and avoiding an excessively large board that may hinder decision-making efficiency.

4-Board Committees:

• Establishing specialized board committees can enhance the effectiveness of the board structure. Committees such as audit, compensation, and nominating/governance committees allow for in-depth examination and focused oversight of specific areas.

• These committees assist the board in fulfilling its responsibilities by providing expertise and recommendations in their respective areas of focus.

5. Board Leadership:

• The leadership structure within the board is crucial for its effectiveness. The separation of roles between the chairperson and CEO (Chief Executive Officer) is considered a best practice to avoid concentration of power.

• A separate chairperson, who is independent and distinct from the CEO, can provide effective oversight and leadership to the board.

6-Board Evaluation:

• Regular board evaluations are essential to assess the performance and effectiveness of the board structure.

• This evaluation can be conducted internally or with the assistance of external consultants.

• The evaluation process helps identify areas for improvement, such as enhancing board dynamics, addressing skills gaps, and ensuring effective decision-making processes. .

7. Board Diversity:

• A diverse board structure contributes to its effectiveness. Diversity in terms of gender, ethnicity, age, expertise, and background brings different perspectives and insights to board discussions.

• It promotes better decision-making, encourages innovation, and reflects the diverse interests of stakeholders.

8. Board Education and Development:

• Continuous education and development programs for board members enhance their effectiveness.

• Providing access to training, workshops, and resources allows board members to stay updated on emerging governance practices, industry trends, and regulatory requirements.

• Ongoing development ensures that board members can effectively fulfill their responsibilities

Design the executive compensation in promoting corporate governance

Designing executive compensation plans that promote corporate governance involves aligning:

i. Incentives with long-term value creation,

ii. Sustainability and

iii. Ethical behavior

Key considerations in design executive compensation

1. Performance Metrics:

• Tie executive compensation to a balanced set of performance metrics that align with the organization's long-term goals and values.

• Beyond financial metrics, include non-financial factors such as ESG performance, customer satisfaction, employee engagement, and innovation.

• This encourages executives to focus on sustainable performance and stakeholder value.

2. Long-Term Incentives:

• Implement long-term incentive plans, such as equity-based compensation, to align executive interests with long-term value creation.

• This can include stock options, restricted stock units, or performance-based equity awards.

• Linking compensation to long-term performance encourages executives to make decisions that support the organization's long-term success.

3. Clawback Provisions:

• Include clawback provisions in executive compensation agreements, allowing the organization to reclaim compensation in the event of financial restatements, misconduct, or material violations of ethical standards.

• Clawback provisions promote accountability and responsible behavior by executives.

4. Risk Alignment:

• Ensure executive compensation plans are designed in a manner that discourages excessive risk-taking.

• Balancing short-term incentives with long-term objectives can help prevent executives from pursuing strategies that prioritize short-term gains at the expense of long-term sustainability.

5. Transparency and Disclosure:

• Make executive compensation practices transparent by providing clear and comprehensive disclosure to stakeholders.

• This includes disclosing the structure of compensation plans, performance metrics, target levels, and actual payouts. Transparent disclosure promotes trust and accountability

6. Shareholder Input:

• Consider incorporating shareholder input into executive compensation decisions.

• This can be done through regular shareholder engagement, "say-on-pay" votes, or advisory votes on executive compensation.

• Seeking shareholder input fosters accountability and aligns compensation practices with shareholder interests.

7. Independent Compensation Committee:

• Establish an independent compensation committee within the board of directors.

• This committee should consist of independent directors who are responsible for overseeing and approving executive compensation.

• Independence ensures objective decision-making and avoids conflicts of interest.

8. Benchmarking and Peer Comparison:

• Conduct thorough benchmarking analyses to ensure executive compensation is competitive within the industry and aligned with the organization's performance.

• Compare compensation practices against peer companies of similar size and industry to maintain a reasonable and justifiable compensation structure

9. Ethical Considerations:

Incorporate ethical guidelines into executive compensation plans. This can include requirements for compliance with laws, regulations, and ethical standards, as well as specific provisions addressing ethical conduct, diversity and inclusion, and responsible governance practices.

10. Regular Review and Evaluation:

• Continuously review and evaluate executive compensation plans to ensure they remain aligned with corporate governance goals.

• Regularly assess the effectiveness of compensation structures in driving long-term value creation, ethical behavior, and sustainable performance.

Strategies for engaging with shareholders and addressing shareholder activism

Strategies for engaging with shareholders

1. Proactive Communication:

• Foster open and transparent communication with shareholders on a regular basis.

• Provide timely and accurate information through various channels, such as investor presentations, annual reports, and regulatory filings.

• Proactively share updates on strategic initiatives, financial performance, and governance practices to keep shareholders informed.

2. Shareholder Outreach Programs:

• Develop formal shareholder outreach programs to engage with institutional investors, asset managers, and proxy advisors.

• Conduct one-on-one meetings, investor conferences, and roadshows to discuss the company's strategy, governance practices, and performance.

• Seek feedback and address any concerns or questions raised by shareholders.

3. Proxy Statement Enhancement:

• Enhance the proxy statement to effectively communicate the company's governance practices and executive compensation plans.

• Clearly explain the rationale behind governance decisions, demonstrate alignment with shareholder interests, and provide detailed information on the qualifications and independence of board members.

• Clear and transparent proxy statements can help build trust and support among shareholders.

4. Shareholder Engagement Policies:

• Develop and implement formal shareholder engagement policies that outline the company's commitment to engaging with shareholders.

• These policies can include guidelines on frequency and methods of engagement, the scope of topics for discussion, and the responsibilities of management and the board in engaging with shareholders.

• Shareholder engagement policies demonstrate the company's proactive approach to communication and responsiveness.

5. Regular Investor Meetings:

• Conduct regular meetings with key institutional investors and other significant shareholders.

• These meetings provide opportunities to understand their perspectives, address concerns, and seek alignment on important matters.

• Building relationships with key shareholders can help mitigate potential activism and foster a supportive shareholder base.

6. Environmental, Social, and Governance (ESG) Engagement:

• Given the increasing focus on ESG factors, engage with shareholders on ESG-related topics.

• Share the company's ESG initiatives, performance, and targets. Seek input on ESG practices and consider shareholder proposals aligned with ESG goals.

• Engaging on ESG issues demonstrates the company's commitment to sustainability and responsible business practices.

7. Board Refreshment and Diversity:

• Proactively address concerns around board composition and diversity by regularly assessing board effectiveness and refreshing board membership when necessary.

• Consider the skills, experiences, and diversity needed on the board to align with evolving business strategies and stakeholder expectations.

• Demonstrating a commitment to board refreshment and diversity can help address shareholder activism.

8. Robust Risk Management:

• Implement robust risk management practices to mitigate potential risks and address shareholder concerns.

• Regularly assess and disclose the company's risk profile, risk mitigation strategies, and governance processes.

• Addressing potential risks and demonstrating effective risk management can help alleviate shareholder concerns and enhance confidence in the company's governance practices.

9. Proxy Solicitation and Voting Support:

• Work with proxy solicitation firms and proxy advisors to secure support for key governance proposals and executive compensation plans.

• Develop persuasive arguments, engage in discussions, and seek their recommendations to influence voting decisions.

• Building relationships with proxy advisory firms and actively engaging with them can be critical in addressing shareholder activism.

10. Continuous Improvement:

• Regularly evaluate and refine shareholder engagement strategies based on feedback and changing market dynamics.

• Stay informed about emerging governance trends, regulatory developments, and best practices in shareholder engagement.

• Continuously assess the effectiveness of engagement efforts and adapt strategies accordingly

Governance Compliance Checklist

How well is your board or committee of management performing?

Complete this self-assessment checklist. You can use the results to assess your board of committee of management's governance strengths and weaknesses. Throughout this checklist, when referring to the term 'board', it also refers to 'committee of management'.

A list of key terms can be found in the appendix of this document.

Question	Yes	No	What actions do you need to take to correct the current situation?
1. Does your association review at least annually, the structure of your board to ensure that it complies to the principles of best practice corporate governance as specified by your state?			
2. Does your association record independent vs. interested club or association directors?			
3. Does your organisation review its membership?			
4. Does your organisation have a procedure for the appointment and retirement of members of the board and particularly for independent directors?			
5. Are your association directors able to seek independent professional advice?			
6. Do you pay your association directors compensation?			
7. Is your association board able to identify areas of significant risks in and for your club or association?			
8. Does your organisation have a policy on appropriate ethical standards for your association directors?			
9. Does your association have a register for declarations of conflicts of interest?			

Switzerland: A Global Leader in Corporate Governance and Accountability

Switzerland is often regarded as one of the best examples of a country with strong corporate governance practices. Here's how Switzerland excels in corporate governance:

1. **High Standards of Transparency and Accountability**:

Switzerland is known for its strict regulations surrounding corporate transparency:

- **Financial Reporting**: Swiss companies are required to disclose detailed financial statements that follow international standards. Publicly traded companies are subject to rigorous auditing processes and are obliged to share comprehensive information with shareholders and stakeholders.
- **Shareholder Rights**: Swiss corporate law places a high emphasis on the rights of shareholders, ensuring they have a say in corporate decisions through voting, especially in annual general meetings (AGMs). Shareholders can challenge management decisions if necessary, and they have the right to receive accurate and timely information.

2. **Independent Boards**:

Switzerland promotes strong corporate governance through the structure of independent boards:

- **Board Composition**: Swiss companies typically have boards with a mix of independent members, which ensures that decisions are made with objectivity and in the best interest of shareholders.
- **Separation of CEO and Chairman**: In many Swiss companies, the roles of CEO and Chairman are separated, reducing the potential for conflicts of interest and ensuring proper oversight of executive management.

3. **Strong Legal Framework**:

The Swiss legal system enforces a solid corporate governance framework:

- **Code of Best Practice**: Switzerland has developed the "Swiss Code of Best Practice for Corporate Governance," which is followed by many companies as a guideline for governance practices. The Code provides recommendations for the roles of directors, executive pay, financial disclosures, and shareholder relations.
- **Regulatory Bodies**: Regulatory bodies, such as the Swiss Financial Market Supervisory Authority (FINMA), ensure that companies adhere to governance standards and regulations, helping to maintain trust in the financial system.

4. **Ethical Business Practices**:

Switzerland places a strong emphasis on ethical conduct in business:

- **Anti-Corruption Measures**: Switzerland enforces strict anti-corruption laws, ensuring that businesses operate with integrity and fairness. Companies are expected to adopt strong internal controls to prevent fraud and other unethical behaviors.
- **Sustainability and Responsibility**: Many Swiss companies, especially in industries like banking and finance, integrate sustainability and social responsibility into their corporate strategies, aligning with international ESG (Environmental, Social, Governance) standards.

5. **Executive Compensation and Accountability**:

Swiss corporate governance holds executives accountable for their actions and decisions:

- **Shareholder Influence on Executive Pay**: Shareholders in Switzerland have the right to vote on executive compensation packages, providing oversight on excessive pay and ensuring alignment with company performance.
- **Performance-Based Incentives**: Executive compensation in Switzerland is often tied to company performance, ensuring that executives are incentivized to create long-term value for shareholders.

6. **Stakeholder Considerations**:

Swiss governance considers not just shareholders, but other stakeholders:

- **Balancing Interests**: Swiss corporate governance focuses on balancing the interests of shareholders, employees, customers, and the wider community. This approach encourages responsible business practices that contribute to sustainable growth and long-term value creation.

Switzerland stands out as a model for corporate governance due to its transparency, independence of boards, strong legal framework, ethical practices, and shareholder protections. Its regulatory environment ensures that companies operate responsibly and accountably, making Switzerland an example of best practices in corporate governance globally.

Module 5
ESG Reporting and Communication

Principles of ESG reporting and communication

1. Transparency

• Transparency is the foundation of ESG reporting and communication.

• It involves providing accurate, reliable, and comprehensive information about an organization's ESG practices and performance.

• Transparent reporting enables stakeholders to understand the company's impacts, risks, and opportunities, fostering trust and informed decision-making.

2. Materiality:

• Materiality refers to the identification and disclosure of ESG issues that are significant to a company and its stakeholders.

• It involves assessing the relevance and impact of various ESG factors on the organization's operations, strategy, and financial performance.

• Reporting on material issues helps stakeholders understand the most critical sustainability challenges facing the company.

3. Stakeholder Engagement:

• Engaging with stakeholders is vital for effective ESG reporting and communication.

• It involves actively seeking input, feedback, and dialogue with stakeholders to understand their perspectives, expectations, and concerns.

• Engaging stakeholders ensures that ESG reporting captures their interests and helps build strong relationships based on trust and collaboration.

4. Consistency:

• Consistency ensures that ESG reporting and communication are conducted in a standardized and comparable manner over time.

• It involves following recognized reporting frameworks, such as GRI, SASB, or TCFD, to provide consistency across different reporting periods and enable benchmarking between companies.

• Consistent reporting enables stakeholders to track an organization's progress and performance over time.

5. Balance:

• ESG reporting and communication should present a balanced view of an organization's performance, both highlighting achievements and addressing challenges.

• It is essential to provide a fair representation of efforts made to address ESG issues while acknowledging areas for improvement.

6. Contextualization:

• Contextualization involves providing a clear understanding of the broader context in which an organization operates.

• It includes explaining industry-specific challenges, regional or global trends, regulatory frameworks, and market dynamics that influence the company's ESG performance.

• Contextualization helps stakeholders assess the relevance and significance of reported information within the larger landscape.

7. Clarity and Accessibility:

• ESG reporting and communication should be clear, concise, and easily understandable for a wide range of stakeholders.

• The use of plain language, visual aids, and meaningful metrics can enhance accessibility.

• Clear communication enables stakeholders to grasp the information quickly and make informed decisions regarding the organization's ESG practices

Global Reporting Initiative (GRI)

System of GRI Standards

The objective of sustainability reporting using the GRI Sustainability

• GRI Standards to provide transparency on how an organization contributes or aims to contribute to sustainable development.

• The GRI Standards enable an organization to publicly disclose its most significant impacts on the economy, environment, and people, including impacts on their human rights and how the organization manages these impacts.

• This enhances transparency on the organization's impacts and increases organizational accountability

• The GRI Standards are structured as a system of interrelated standards that are organized into three series: Universal Standards: GRI 1, GRI 2 and GRI 3

Universal Standards: GRI 1, GRI 2, GRI3

GRI 1: Foundation 2021	GRI 2: General Disclosures 2021	GRI 3: Material Topics 2021
• It specifies the requirements that the organization must comply with to report in accordance with the GRI Standards. The organization begins using the GRI Standards by consulting GRI 1	• It contains disclosures that the organization uses to provide information about its reporting practices and other organizational details, such as its activities, governance, and policies	• It guides how to determine material topics. It also contains disclosures that the organization uses to report information about its process of determining material topics, its list of material topics, and how it manages each topic
• Requirements and principles for using the GRI Standards	• Disclosures about the reporting organization	• Disclosures and guidance about the organization's material topics

GRI 1: Foundation 2021

GRI 1: Key Concepts of GRI

• Understanding how these 4 concepts are applied in the GRI Standards is essential for those who collect and prepare information for reporting and those who interpret information that is reported using the Standards.

Four key concepts of GRI are:

Concept 1-Impact,

Concept 2- Material topics,

Concept 3-Due diligence,

Concept 4- Stakeholder.

• The purpose of the Standards is to enable organizations to report information about their most significant impacts on the economy, environment, and people, including impacts on their human rights, in the GRI Standards these are referred to as material topics. Due diligence and stakeholder engagement help organizations identify their most significant impacts

GRI 1: Concept 1: IMPACT

• In the GRI Standards, impact refers to the effect an organization has or could have on the economy, environment, and people, including effects on their human rights, as a result of the organization's activities or business relationships.

• The impacts can be actual or potential, negative or positive, short-term or long-term, intended or unintended, and reversible or irreversible.

• These impacts indicate the organization's contribution, negative or positive, to sustainable development.

GRI 1: Concept 2: Material Topics

• An organization may identify many impacts on which to report.

• When using the GRI Standards, the organization prioritizes reporting on those topics that represent its most significant impacts on the economy, environment, and people, including impacts on their human rights. In the GRI Standards, these are the organization's material topics.

• Examples of material topics are anti-corruption, occupational health and safety, or water and effluents.

• A topic need not be limited to impacts on the economy, the environment, or people; it can cover impacts across all three dimensions.

GRI 1: Concept 3: Due Diligence

• In the GRI Standards, due diligence refers to the process through which an organization identifies, prevents, mitigates, and accounts for how it addresses its actual and potential negative impacts on the economy, environment, and people, including impacts on their human rights.

• The organization should address potential negative impacts through prevention or mitigation. It should address actual negative impacts through remediation in cases where the organization identifies it has caused or contributed to those impacts.

• The way the organization is involved with negative impacts (i.e., whether it causes or contributes to the impacts, or whether the impacts are directly linked to its business relationships) determines how the organization should address the impacts.

GRI 1: Concept 4: Stakeholders

• Stakeholders are individuals or groups that have interests that are affected or could be affected by an organization's activities.

• Common categories of stakeholders for organizations are business partners, civil society organizations, consumers, customers, employees and other workers, governments, local communities, non-governmental organizations, shareholders and other investors, suppliers, trade unions, and vulnerable groups.

• In the GRI Standards, an interest (or 'stake') is something of value to an individual or group, which can be affected by the activities of an organization.

• Stakeholders can have more than one interest. Not all interests are of equal importance and they do not all need to be treated equally. Human rights have a particular status as an entitlement of all people under international law. The most acute impacts the organization can have on people are those that negatively affect their human rights

GRI 1: Foundation 2021

Principles of GRI Reporting and Disclosure (GRI 1: Foundation 2021)		
No	Principles	Requirement
1	Accuracy	The organization shall report information that is correct and sufficiently detailed to allow an assessment of the organization's impacts.
2	Balance	The organization shall report information in an unbiased way and provide a fair representation of the organization's negative and positive impacts.
3	Clarity	The organization shall present information in a way that is accessible and understandable
4	Comparability	The organization shall select, compile, and report information consistently to enable an analysis of changes in the organization's impacts over time and an analysis of these impacts relative to those of other organizations.
5	Completeness	The organization shall provide sufficient information to enable an assessment of the organization's impacts during the reporting period.
6	Sustainability Context	The organization shall report information about its impacts in the wider context of sustainable development.
7	Timeless	The organization shall report information on a regular schedule and make it available in time for information users to make decisions.
8	Verifiability	The organization shall gather, record, compile, and analyze information in such a way that the information can be examined to establish its quality

GRI 1: How to report according to GRI Standards?

• Reporting in accordance with the GRI Standards enables an organization to provide a comprehensive picture of its most significant impacts on the economy, environment, and people, including impacts on their human rights, and how it manages these impacts. This allows information users to make informed assessments and decisions about the organization's impacts and its contribution to sustainable development.

• The organization must comply with all nine requirements in this section to report in accordance with the GRI

• Standards. If the organization does not comply with all nine requirements, it cannot claim that it has prepared the reported information in accordance with the GRI Standards

GRI 1: Compulsory meeting all 9 requirements

• Requirement 1: Apply the reporting principles

• Requirement 2: Report the disclosures in GRI 2: General Disclosures 2021

• Requirement 3: Determine material topics

• Requirement 4: Report the disclosures in GRI 3: Material Topics 2021

• Requirement 5: Report disclosures from the GRI Topic Standards for each material topic

• Requirement 6: Provide reasons for omission for disclosures and requirements that the organization cannot comply with

• Requirement 7: Publish a GRI content index

• Requirement 8: Provide a statement of use: [Name of organization] has reported in accordance with the GRI Standards for the period [reporting period start and end dates].

• Requirement 9: Notify GRI. The organization shall notify GRI of the use of the GRI Standards and the statement of use by sending an email to reportregistration@globalreporting.org.

GRI 2: General Disclosures 2021

Area 1: The organization and its reporting practices

• The disclosures in this section provide an overview of the organization, its sustainability reporting practices, and the entities included in its sustainability reporting

• Disclosure 2-1 Organizational details

• Disclosure 2-2 Entities included in the organization's sustainability reporting

• Disclosure 2-3 Reporting period, frequency and contact point

• Disclosure 2-4 Restatements of information

• Disclosure 2-5 External assurance that includes the description of policy and practice for seeking external assurance, including whether and how the highest governance body and senior executives are involved.

Area 2: Activities and workers

• The disclosures in this section provide an overview of the organization's activities, employees, and other workers.

• Disclosure 2-6 Activities, value chain and other business relationships

• Disclosure 2-7 Employees

• Disclosure 2-8 Workers who are not employees

Area 3: Governance

• The disclosures in this section provide information about the organization's governance structure, composition, knowledge, roles, and remuneration

• Disclosure 2-9 Governance structure and composition

• Disclosure 2-10 Nomination and selection of the highest governance body

• Disclosure 2-11 Chair of the highest governance body

• Disclosure 2-12 Role of the highest governance body in overseeing the

• management of impacts

• Disclosure 2-13 Delegation of responsibility for managing impacts

• Disclosure 2-14 Role of the highest governance body in sustainability reporting

• Disclosure 2-15 Conflicts of interest

• Disclosure 2-16 Communication of critical concerns

• Disclosure 2-17 Collective knowledge of the highest governance body

• Disclosure 2-18 Evaluation of the performance of the highest governance body

• Disclosure 2-19 Remuneration policies

• Disclosure 2-20 Process to determine remuneration

• Disclosure 2-21 Annual total compensation ratio

Area 4: Strategy, Policies and Practices

• The disclosures in this section provide information about the organization's sustainable development strategy and its policies and practices for responsible business conduct. The disclosures are based on expectations for businesses contained in authoritative intergovernmental instruments

• Disclosure 2-22 Statement on sustainable development strategy

• Disclosure 2-23 Policy commitments

• Disclosure 2-24 Embedding policy commitments

• Disclosure 2-25 Processes to remediate negative impacts

• Disclosure 2-26 Mechanisms for seeking advice and raising concerns

• Disclosure 2-27 Compliance with laws and regulations

• Disclosure 2-28 Membership associations

Area 5: Stakeholder Engagement

• The disclosures in this section provide information about the organization's stakeholder engagement practices, including how it engages in collective bargaining with employees

• Disclosure 2-29 Approach to stakeholder engagement. Describe its approach to engaging with stakeholders,

• Disclosure 2-30 Collective bargaining agreements. Report the percentage of total employees covered by collective bargaining agreements

GRI 3: Material Topics 2021

Material Topics

Question 1: What are the material topics?

Answer: Material topics are topics that represent the organization's most significant impacts on the economy, environment, and people, including impacts on their human rights

Question 2: How to determine material topics?

Answer: There are 4 step

Step 1. Understand the organization's context

Step 2. Identify actual and potential impacts

Step 3. Assess the significance of the impacts

Step 4. Prioritize the most significant impacts for reporting

Figure 2. Process to determine material topics

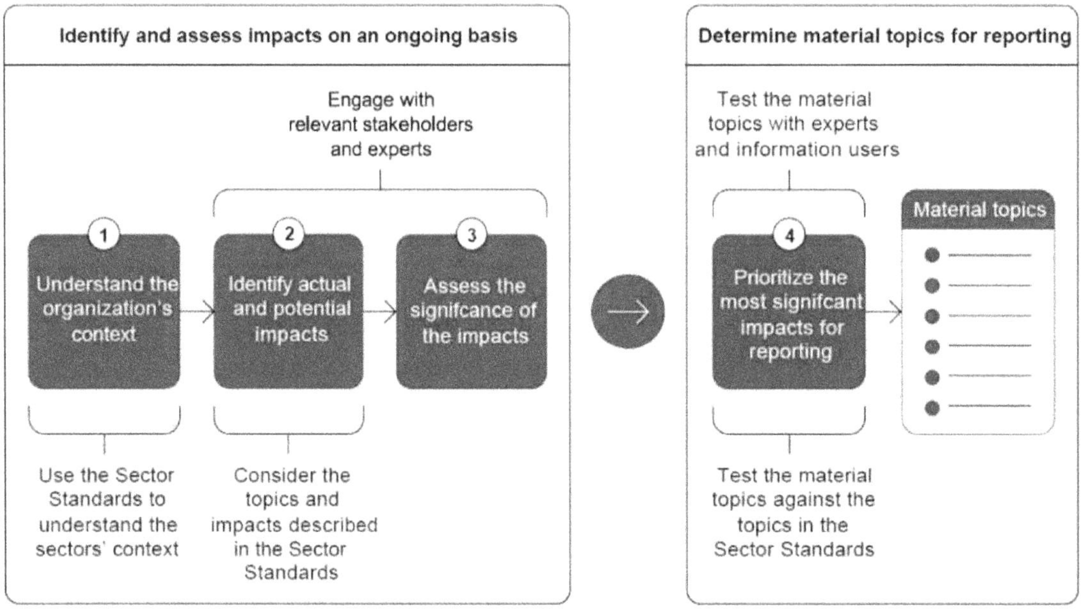

Step 1. Understand the organization's context

• In this step, the organization creates an initial high-level overview of its activities and business relationships, the sustainability context in which these occur, and an overview of its stakeholders. This provides the organization with critical information for identifying its actual and potential impacts.

• The organization should consider the activities, business relationships, stakeholders, and sustainability context of all the entities it controls or has an interest in (e.g., subsidiaries, joint ventures, affiliates), including minority interests

Step 2. Identify actual and potential impacts

• In this step, the organization identifies its actual and potential impacts on the economy, environment, and people, including impacts on their human rights, across the organization's activities and business relationships.

• Actual impacts are those that have already occurred, and potential impacts are those that could occur but have not yet occurred.

• These impacts include negative and positive impacts, short-term and long-term impacts, intended and unintended impacts, and reversible and irreversible impacts.

Step 3. Assess the significance of the impacts •

The organization may identify many actual and potential impacts. In this step, the organization assesses the significance of its identified impacts to prioritize them.

• Prioritization enables the organization to take action to address the impacts and also to determine its material topics for reporting. Prioritizing impacts for action is relevant where it is not feasible to address all impacts at once.

• Assessing the significance of the impacts involves quantitative and qualitative analysis. How significant an impact is will be specific to the organization and will be influenced by the sectors in which it operates, and its business relationships, among other factors.

Step 4. Prioritize the most significant impacts for reporting

• In this step, to determine its material topics for reporting, the organization prioritizes its impacts based on their significance.

• The organization should test its selection of material topics against the topics in the applicable GRI Sector Standards.

• This helps the organization ensure that it has not overlooked any topics that are likely to be material for its sectors.

• The organization's highest governance body should review and approve the list of material topics. If such a body does not exist, a senior executive or group of senior executives in the organization should approve the list

Task Force on Climate-Related Financial Disclosure (TCFD)

Concurrent with the release of its 2023 status report on October 12, 2023, the TCFD has fulfilled its remit and disbanded. The IFRS Foundation to take over the monitoring of the progress of companies' climate-related disclosures

TCFD - 7 Principles of Effective Disclosure

1. Disclosures should represent relevant information

2. Disclosures should be specific and complete

3. Disclosures should be clear, balanced and untestable

4. Disclosures should be consistent over time

5. Disclosures should be comparable among the companies within a sector, industry, or portfolio

6. Disclosures should be reliable, verifiable and objective

7. Disclosures should be provided on a timely basis

Core Elements of Recommended Climate-Related Financial Disclosures (TCFD)

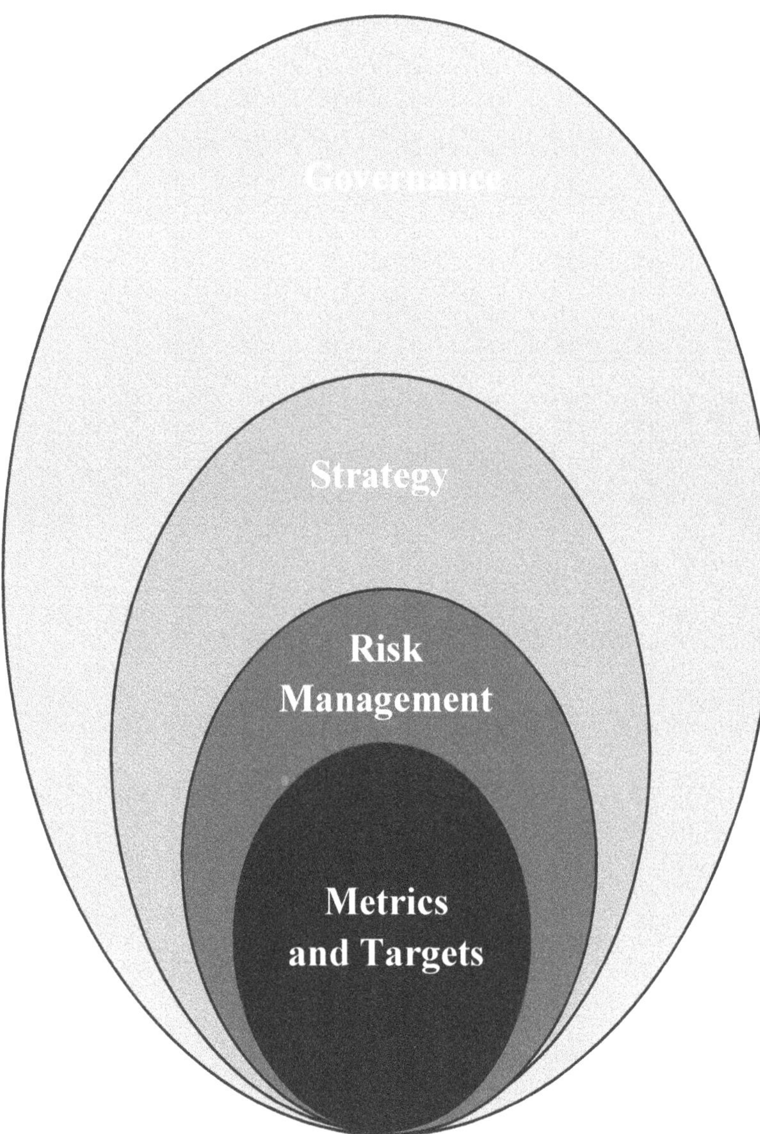

Governance

The Organization's governance around climate-related risks and opportunities

Strategy

The actual and potential impacts of climate-related risks and opportunities on the organizations businesses, strategy and financial planning

Risk Management

The processes used by the organization to identify, assess, and manage climate-related risks

Metrics and Targets

The metrics and targets used to assess and manage relevant climate-related risks and opportunities

TCFD: Governance Disclosures

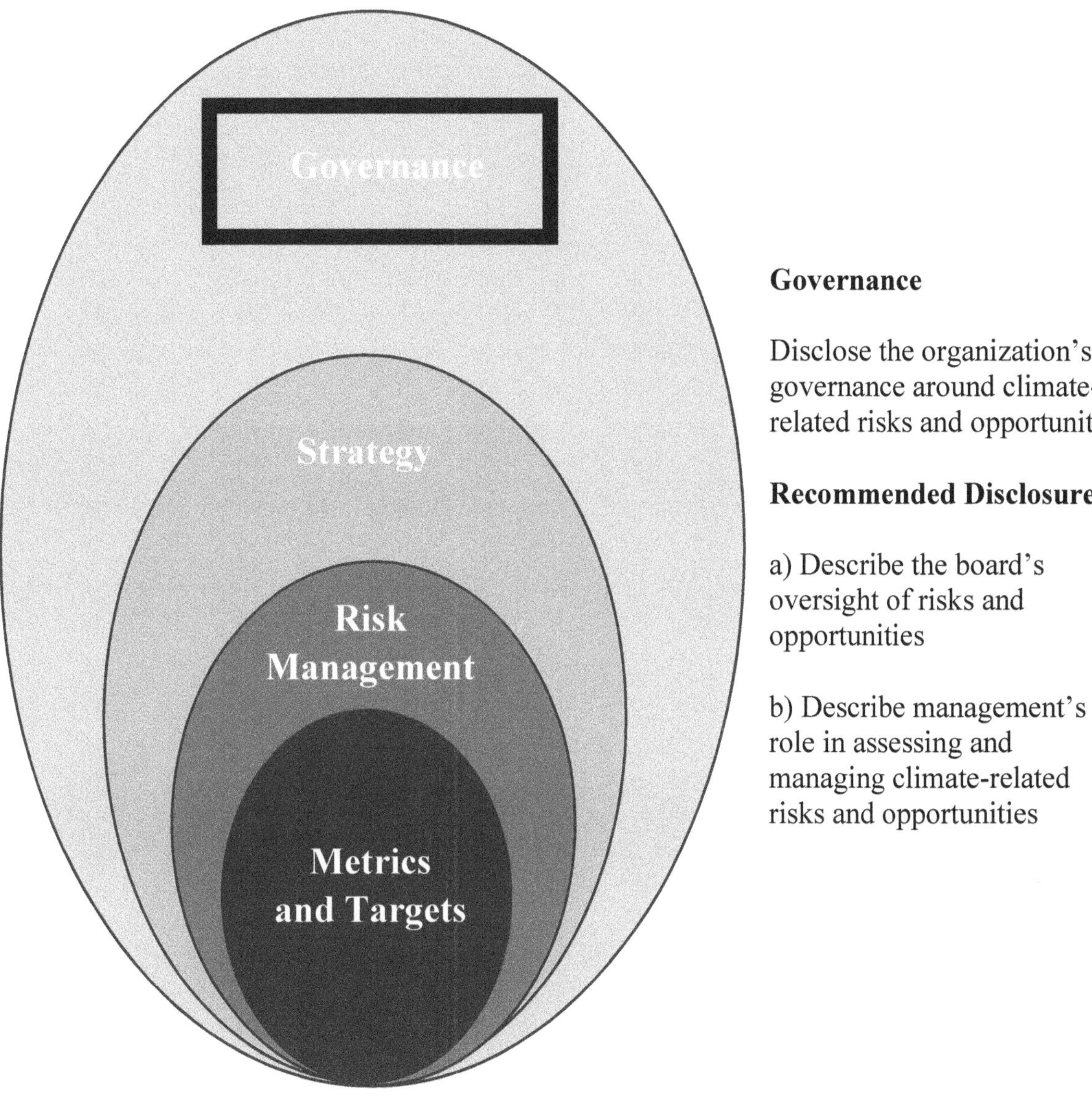

Governance

Disclose the organization's governance around climate-related risks and opportunities

Recommended Disclosures

a) Describe the board's oversight of risks and opportunities

b) Describe management's role in assessing and managing climate-related risks and opportunities

• Investors, lenders, insurance underwriters, and other users of climate-related financial disclosures (collectively referred to as "investors and other stakeholders") are interested in understanding the role an organization's board plays in overseeing climate-related issues as well as management's role in assessing and managing those issues.

• Such information supports evaluations of whether material climate-related issues receive appropriate board and management attention

Governance Disclosures

Recommended Disclosure a)	Guidance for All Sectors
Describe the board's oversight of climate-related risks and opportunities.	In describing the board's oversight of climate-related issues, organizations should consider including a discussion of the following: - Processes and frequency by which the board and/or board committees (e.g., audit, risk, or other committees) are informed about climate-related issues; - Whether the board and/or board committees consider climate-related issues when reviewing and guiding strategy, major plans of action, risk management policies, annual budgets, and business plans as well as setting the organization's performance objectives, monitoring implementation and performance, and overseeing major capital expenditures, acquisitions, and divestitures; - How the board monitors and oversees progress against goals and targets for addressing climate-related issues.

Recommended Disclosure b)	Guidance for All Sectors
Describe management's role in assessing and managing climate-related risks and opportunities.	In describing management's role related to the assessment and management of climate-related issues, organizations should consider including the following information: - Whether the organization has assigned climate-related responsibilities to management-level positions or committees; and, if so, whether such management positions or committees report to the board or a committee of the board and whether those responsibilities include assessing and/or managing climate-related issues; - A description of the associated organizational structure(s); - Processes by which management is informed about climate-related issues; and - How management (through specific positions and/or management committees) monitors climate-related issues.

TCFD: Strategy Disclosures

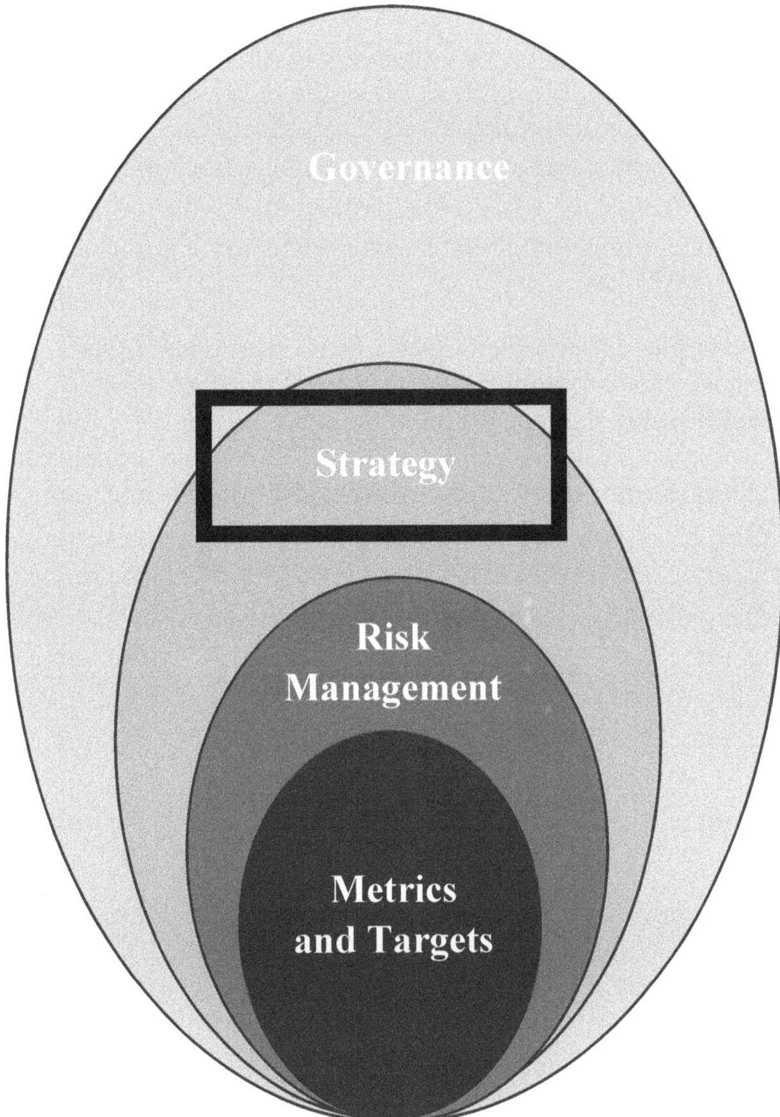

Strategy

The actual and potential impacts of climate-related risks and opportunities on the organizations businesses, strategy and financial planning

Recommended Disclosures

a) Describe the climate-related risks and opportunities the organization has identified over short, medium and long terms

b) Describe the impact of risks and opportunities on the organization's business, strategy and financial planning

c) Describe the resilience of the organization's strategy, taking into consideration different climate related scenario including a 2 deg C or lower the scenario

• Investors and other stakeholders need to understand how climate-related issues may affect an organization's businesses, strategy, and financial planning over the short, medium, and long term.

• Such information is used to inform expectations about the future performance of an organization.

Strategy Disclosure

Recommended Disclosure a)	Guidance for All Sectors
Describe the climate-related risks and opportunities the organization has identified over the short, medium, and long term.	Organizations should provide the following information: - A description of what they consider to be the relevant short-, medium-, and long-term time horizons, taking into consideration the useful life of the organization's assets or infrastructure and the fact that climate-related issues often manifest themselves over the medium and longer terms; - A description of the specific climate-related issues potentially arising in each time horizon (short, medium, and long term) that could have a material financial impact on the organization; and - A description of the process(es) used to determine which risks and opportunities could have a material financial impact on the organization.

Strategy Disclosure

Recommended Disclosure b)	Guidance for All Sectors
Describe the impact of climate-related risks and opportunities on the organization's businesses, strategy, and financial planning.	Building on recommended disclosure (a), organizations should discuss how identified climate-related issues have affected their businesses, strategy, and financial planning. Organizations should consider including the impact on their businesses, strategy, and financial planning in the following areas: - Products and services - Supply chain and/or value chain - Adaptation and mitigation activities - Investment in research and development - Operations (including types of operations and location of facilities) - Acquisitions or divestments - Access to capital Organizations should describe how climate-related issues serve as an input to their financial planning process, the time period(s) used, and how these risks and opportunities are prioritized. Organizations' disclosures should reflect a holistic picture of the interdependencies among the factors that affect their ability to create value over time. Organizations should describe the impact of climate-related issues on their financial performance (e.g., revenues, costs) and financial position (e.g., assets, liabilities). If climate-related scenarios were used to inform the organization's strategy and financial planning, such scenarios should be described. Organizations that have made GHG emissions reduction commitments, operate in jurisdictions that have made such commitments, or have agreed to meet investor expectations regarding GHG emissions reductions should describe their plans for transitioning to a low-carbon economy, which could include GHG emissions targets and specific activities intended to reduce GHG emissions in their operations and value chain or to otherwise support the transition.

Strategy Disclosure

Recommended Disclosure c)	Guidance for All Sectors
Describe the resilience of the organization's strategy, taking into consideration different climate-related scenarios, including a 2°C or lower scenario.	Organizations should describe how resilient their strategies are to climate-related risks and opportunities, taking into consideration a transition to a low-carbon economy consistent with a 2°C or lower scenario and, where relevant to the organization, scenarios consistent with increased physical climate-related risks. Organizations should consider discussing: - where they believe their strategies may be affected by climate-related risks and opportunities; - how their strategies might change to address such potential risks and opportunities; - the potential impact of climate-related issues on financial performance (e.g., revenues, costs) and financial position (e.g., assets, liabilities); - the climate-related scenarios and associated time horizon(s) considered.

TCFD: Risk Management Disclosures

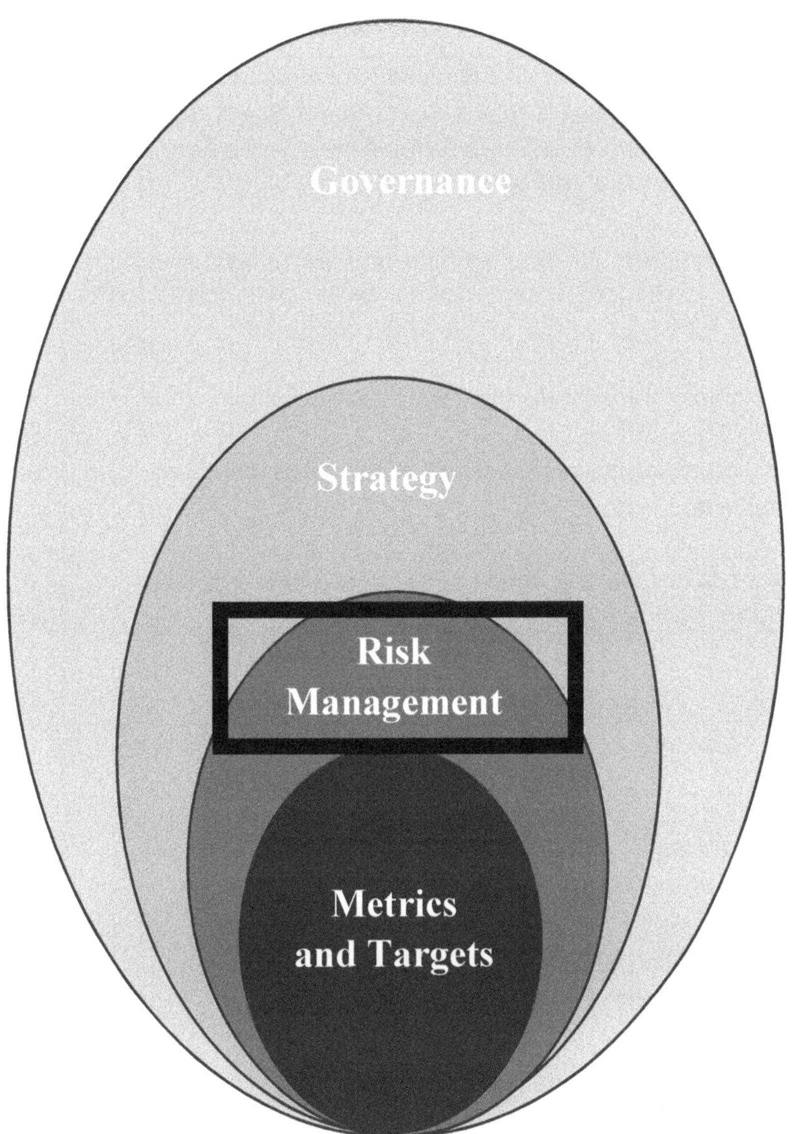

Risk Management

Disclose how the organization identifies, assesses and manages climate-related risks

Recommended Disclosures

a) Describe the organization's processes for identifying and assessing the climate-related risks

b) Describe the organization's processes for managing the climate-related risks

c) Describe how processes for identifying, assessing and managing climate-related risks are integrated with organization's overall risks management

• Investors and other stakeholders need to understand how an organization's climate-related risks are identified, assessed, and managed and whether those processes are integrated in existing risk management processes.

• Such information supports users of climate-related financial disclosures in evaluating the organization's overall risk profile and risk management activities

Risk Management Disclosures

Recommended Disclosure	Guidance for All Sectors
Describe the organization's processes for identifying and assessing climate-related risks.	Organizations should describe their risk management processes for identifying and assessing climate-related risks. An important aspect of this description is how organizations determine the relative significance of climate-related risks in relation to other risks. Organizations should describe whether they consider existing and emerging regulatory requirements related to climate change (e.g., limits on emissions) as well as other relevant factors considered. Organizations should also consider disclosing the following: - Processes for assessing the potential size and scope of identified climate-related risks. - Definitions of risk terminology used or references to existing risk classification frameworks used.

Recommended Disclosure	Guidance for All Sectors
Describe the organization's processes for managing climate-related risks.	Organizations should describe their processes for managing climate-related risks, including how they make decisions to mitigate, transfer, accept, or control those risks. In addition, organizations should describe their processes for prioritizing climate-related risks, including how materiality determinations are made within their organizations.

Recommended Disclosure	Guidance for All Sectors
Describe how processes for identifying, assessing, and managing climate-related risks are integrated into the organization's overall risk management.	Organizations should describe how their processes for identifying, assessing, and managing climate-related risks are integrated into their overall risk management.

TCFD: Metrics & Target Disclosure

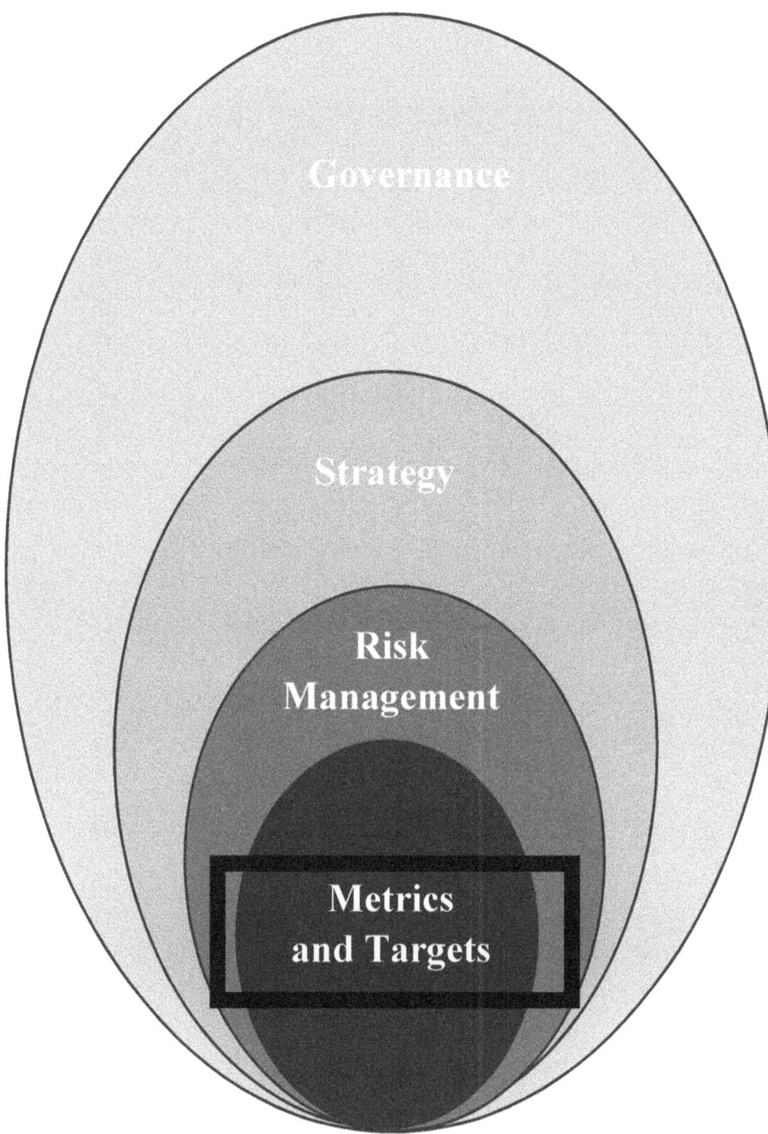

Matrics and Targets

Disclose the matrics and targets used to assess and manage relevant climate-related risks and opportunities where such information are material.

Recommended Disclosures

a) Disclose the matrics used by organization to assess the climate-related risks and opportunities in line with its strategy and risks management process

b) Disclose Scope 1, Scope 2 if appreciate Scope 3.Greenhouse Gas (GHG) emission and the related risks

c) Describe the targets used by the organization to manage climate-related risks and opportunities and performance against targets

• Investors and other stakeholders need to understand how an organization measures and monitors its climate-related risks and opportunities.

• Access to the metrics and targets used by an organization allows investors and other stakeholders to better assess the organization's potential risk-adjusted returns, ability to meet financial obligations, general exposure to climate-related issues, and progress in managing or adapting to those issues.

Metrics Targets Disclosures

Recommended Disclosures (a)

Disclose the matrics used by organization to assess the climate-related risks and opportunities in line with its strategy and risks management process

• Organizations should consider including metrics on climate-related risks associated with water, energy, land use, and waste management where relevant and applicable.

• Where climate-related issues are material, organizations should consider describing whether and how related performance metrics are incorporated into remuneration policies.

• Where relevant, organizations should provide their internal carbon prices as well as climate-related opportunity metrics such as revenue from products and services designed for a low-carbon economy.

• Metrics should be provided for historical periods to allow for trend analysis.

• In addition, where not apparent, organizations should describe the methodologies used to calculate or estimate climate-related metrics.

Recommended Disclosures (b)

Disclose Scope 1, Scope 2 if appreciate Scope 3.Greenhouse Gas (GHG) emission and the related risks

Recommended Disclosure	Guidance for All Sectors
Disclose Scope 1, Scope 2, and, if appropriate, Scope 3 greenhouse gas (GHG) emissions, and the related risks.	Organizations should provide their Scope 1 and Scope 2 GHG emissions independent of a materiality assessment, and, if appropriate, Scope 3 GHG emissions and the related risks. All organizations should consider disclosing Scope 3 GHG emissions. GHG emissions should be calculated in line with the GHG Protocol methodology to allow for aggregation and comparability across organizations and jurisdictions. As appropriate, organizations should consider providing related, generally accepted industry-specific GHG efficiency ratios. GREENHOUSE GAS (GHG) EMISSIONS SCOPE LEVELS: - Scope 1 refers to all direct GHG emissions. - Scope 2 refers to indirect GHG emissions from consumption of purchased electricity, heat, or steam. - Scope 3 refers to other indirect emissions not covered in Scope 2 that occur in the value chain of the reporting company, including both upstream and downstream emissions. Scope 3 emissions could include the extraction and production of purchased materials and fuels, transport-related activities in vehicles not owned or controlled by the reporting entity, electricity-related activities (e.g., transmission and distribution losses), outsourced activities, and waste disposal.

Recommended Disclosures (c)

Describe the targets used by the organization to manage climate-related risks and opportunities and performance against targets

Guidance for All Sectors

• Organizations should describe their key climate-related targets such as those related to GHG emissions, water usage, energy usage, etc., consistent with the cross-industry, climate-related metric categories where relevant, and in line with anticipated regulatory requirements or market constraints or other goals.

• Other goals may include efficiency or financial goals, financial loss tolerances, avoided GHG emissions through the entire product life cycle, or net revenue goals for products and services designed for a low-carbon economy.

Appendix

(For References)

Additions

- Differentiate the mandatory and voluntary disclosure of ESG information.
- Differentiate different types of ESG reports and their audience and purpose (i.e reporting framework)
- Explain the concept of materiality in ESG Compliance and reporting
- Formulate strategies for collecting, analyzing, and disclosing ESG data and communicating it effectively to stakeholders.
- Key Performance Indicators (KPIs) for Environmental, Social, and Governance (ESG)
- Template for Implementing Global Reporting Initiative (GRI) on ESG Reporting
- Checklist for Implementation Global Reporting Initiative (GRI) on ESG Reporting

(A)

Differentiate the mandatory and voluntary disclosure of ESG information

The differentiation between mandatory and voluntary disclosure of ESG (Environmental, Social, and Governance) information lies in the requirements and obligations surrounding the reporting of such information It's worth noting that the landscape of ESG reporting is evolving, and mandatory requirements are becoming more prevalent in many jurisdictions. Some countries are adopting legislation that makes certain aspects of ESG reporting mandatory for companies, reflecting the growing importance of sustainability and responsible business practices. However, even in the presence of mandatory disclosure requirements, companies may still choose to engage in voluntary reporting to provide more comprehensive and meaningful information to stakeholders.

1. Mandatory Disclosure:

Definition: Mandatory disclosure refers to the legal or regulatory requirements imposed on companies to report specific ESG information.

Basis: These requirements are established by governmental bodies or regulatory authorities at the national, regional, or industry level.

Scope: Mandatory disclosure typically focuses on specific ESG aspects that are deemed critical for regulatory compliance or investor protection.

Examples: In some countries, mandatory ESG reporting requirements may include disclosing greenhouse gas emissions, employee health and safety statistics, board diversity information, executive compensation details, or anti-corruption measures.

• **Enforcement:** Non-compliance with mandatory disclosure requirements can result in penalties, fines, or legal consequences for the company.

2. Voluntary Disclosure:

Definition: Voluntary disclosure refers to the proactive disclosure of ESG information by companies beyond the legally required minimum.

Basis: Voluntary disclosure is driven by an organization's commitment to transparency, stakeholder engagement, and sustainable business practices.

Scope: Voluntary disclosure offers flexibility in terms of the ESG topics and metrics to be reported. It allows companies to go beyond regulatory requirements and disclose a broader range of information that is relevant to their specific industry, operations, and stakeholder interests.

Examples: Voluntary disclosure may include additional ESG performance metrics, goals, initiatives, impact assessments, best practices, case studies, or narrative explanations of the company's sustainability journey.

Motivation: Companies voluntarily disclose ESG information to demonstrate their commitment to sustainability, attract socially responsible investors, build trust with stakeholders, enhance their reputation, and differentiate themselves in the marketplace.

Ultimately, both mandatory and voluntary disclosure of ESG information contribute to greater transparency, accountability, and sustainable business practices. They help stakeholders make informed decisions, hold companies accountable for their impacts, and encourage continuous improvement in ESG performance.

(B)

Differentiate different types of ESG reports and their audience and purpose (i.e reporting framework)

ESG reports come in various formats and cater to different audiences and purposes. The choice of reporting framework depends on factors such as the organization's industry, geographic location, stakeholder expectations, and reporting goals. Here are some common types of ESG reports and their audience and purpose:

Type of Report 1

Sustainability Reports:

Audience: Sustainability reports target a broad range of stakeholders, including investors, employees, customers, communities, NGOs, and the general public.

Purpose: The purpose of sustainability reports is to provide a comprehensive overview of an organization's sustainability performance, initiatives, goals, and impacts. These reports often cover a wide range of ESG topics, including environmental management, social responsibility, governance practices, and economic contributions.

Type of Report 2

Integrated Reports:

Audience: Integrated reports are typically aimed at investors, shareholders, analysts, and financial institutions.

Purpose: Integrated reports seek to provide a holistic view of a company's value creation by integrating financial and non-financial (including ESG) information. These reports emphasize the interrelationships between financial performance, environmental impact, social value, and governance practices.

Type of Report 3

ESG Disclosures in Annual Reports:

Audience: ESG disclosures within annual reports primarily target investors, shareholders, and financial stakeholders.

Purpose: These disclosures are meant to integrate ESG information into the company's annual financial reporting, providing insights into material ESG risks, opportunities, and performance metrics alongside traditional financial data. The aim is to enable investors to make more informed decisions by considering both financial and non-financial aspects.

Type of Report 4

GRI Reports:

Audience: Global Reporting Initiative (GRI) reports target a broad range of stakeholders, including investors, employees, customers, NGOs, regulators, and the general public.

Purpose: GRI is one of the most widely used ESG reporting frameworks. GRI reports provide a structured and standardized approach to reporting on a comprehensive set of ESG indicators. These reports enable organizations to disclose their ESG impacts, commitments, and progress based on the GRI reporting guidelines.

Type of Report

5. SASB Reports:

Audience: Sustainability Accounting Standards Board (SASB) reports primarily target investors, financial analysts, and capital markets.

Purpose: SASB provides industry-specific reporting standards focused on financially material ESG issues. SASB reports aim to facilitate the disclosure of ESG information that is most relevant and decision-useful for investors. They emphasize the connection between ESG performance and financial performance within specific industries.

Type of Report 6

TCFD Reports:

Audience: Task Force on Climate-related Financial Disclosures (TCFD) reports primarily target investors, financial institutions, regulators, and companies exposed to climate-related risks.

Purpose: TCFD reports focus on disclosing climate-related risks and opportunities, providing investors and stakeholders with information to assess an organization's resilience in the face of climate change. These reports align with the TCFD recommendations, which encourage companies to disclose climate-related information within their mainstream financial filings.

(C)

Formulate strategies for collecting, analyzing, and disclosing ESG data and communicating it effectively to stakeholders

Strategy 1

Establish a Robust Data Collection Process:

Identify Relevant Data: Determine the key ESG metrics and indicators that align with your organization's material ESG issues and reporting frameworks.

Data Collection Systems: Implement systems to collect, manage, and store ESG data effectively. This may involve using software solutions, integrating data from various sources, and establishing data governance practices.

Engage Stakeholders: Collaborate with relevant departments, business units, and external stakeholders to gather ESG data. This can include conducting surveys, interviews, audits, or leveraging existing data sources.

Automate Data Collection: Utilize automation tools and technology to streamline data collection processes, reduce manual effort, and improve data accuracy.

Strategy 2

Perform Robust Data Analysis:

Define Performance Indicators: Develop clear performance indicators to measure and track progress on ESG goals. This allows for meaningful analysis and benchmarking over time.

Use Data Analytics Tools: Leverage data analytics tools to identify trends, patterns, and insights from ESG data. This can help uncover correlations and connections between ESG performance and business outcomes.

Conduct Impact Assessments: Analyze the impact of ESG initiatives and actions on the organization, stakeholders, and the environment. This helps assess the effectiveness of sustainability efforts and informs decision-making.

Strategy 3

Disclose ESG Data Effectively:

Select Relevant Reporting Frameworks: Choose appropriate ESG reporting frameworks (e.g., GRI, SASB, TCFD) that align with your organization's industry, reporting goals, and stakeholder expectations.

Provide Contextual Information: Clearly explain the context and significance of reported ESG data. This includes outlining industry specific challenges, trends, and benchmarks to enable stakeholders to understand the performance in a broader context.

Utilize Visual Aids: Use visual aids such as charts, graphs, and infographics to present ESG data in a clear and accessible manner. Visual representations enhance understanding and engagement among stakeholders.

Include Narrative Descriptions: Supplement quantitative data with narrative descriptions that provide qualitative insights into ESG initiatives, challenges, and progress. This storytelling approach adds depth and context to the reported information.

Ensure Accuracy and Verification: Implement internal verification and assurance processes to ensure the accuracy and reliability of reported ESG data. Third-party audits or verification can further enhance the credibility of the disclosed information.

Strategy 4

Tailor Communication to Stakeholder Needs:

Identify Stakeholder Priorities: Understand the information needs and preferences of different stakeholder groups. Tailor the communication of ESG data to address their specific interests, concerns, and knowledge levels.

Use Multiple Channels: Employ a variety of communication channels to reach stakeholders effectively. This can include annual reports, dedicated sustainability reports, company websites, social media, webinars, conferences, and direct engagement.

Foster Two-Way Communication: Encourage dialogue and feedback from stakeholders. Engage in proactive stakeholder engagement activities, such as surveys, focus groups, or stakeholder meetings, to gather insights and strengthen relationships.

Translate Technical Language: Simplify technical terminology and jargon to make ESG information accessible and understandable to a wider audience. Use plain language and avoid excessive complexity.

Key Performance Indicators (KPIs) for Environmental, Social, and Governance (ESG)

Environmental KPIs

No	Area	KPI	Measurement
1	Greenhouse Gas Emissions (GHG)	Total GHG emissions (Scope 1, 2, and 3) in metric tons of CO2 equivalent.	Collect data on direct emissions (Scope 1), indirect emissions from energy consumption (Scope 2), and other indirect emissions (Scope 3) using tools like the GHG Protocol. Use the GHG Protocol tools to collect and calculate emissions data from various sources, including fuel usage records, electricity bills, and supply chain emissions reports.
2	Energy Consumption	Total energy consumption in megawatt-hours (MWh).	Track energy usage from all sources (electricity, natural gas, renewable sources) and record it in energy management systems.
3	Water Usage	Total water withdrawal in cubic meters.	Monitor water meters and usage records to measure the total amount of water withdrawn from all sources.
4	Waste Generation	Total waste generated in metric tons.	Record the weight of waste produced, segregating by type (hazardous, non- hazardous) and disposal method (landfill, recycling, composting).
5	Biodiversity Impact	Number of initiatives to protect and restore Biodiversity	Count the number of projects and initiatives aimed at biodiversity conservation and restoration, and track progress.

Social KPIs

No	Area	KPI	Measurement
1	Employee Diversity	Percentage of employees by gender, age group, and minority status	Analyze HR records to determine the demographic breakdown of the workforce.
2	Health and Safety Incidents	Total number of recordable injuries and illnesses per 100 employees.	Track incident reports and calculate the rate using OSHA or similar regulatory guidelines.
3	Employee Training and Development	Average hours of training per employee per year.	Record training sessions and hours completed by each employee, using learning management systems (LMS).
4	Community Engagement	Total number of community projects and volunteer hours	Track the number of community projects supported and volunteer hours logged by employees.
5	Human Rights Practices	Number of human rights violations reported.	Monitor and record any incidents of human rights violations through internal reporting systems.

Governance KPIs

No	Area	KPI	Measurement
1	Board Diversity	Percentage of board members by gender and minority status.	Analyze board composition records to determine the demographic breakdown.
2	Executive Compensation Alignment	Percentage of executive compensation tied to ESG performance.	Review executive compensation packages to assess the proportion linked to ESG-related targets.
3	ESG Risk Management	Number of ESG risks identified and mitigated.	Use risk management frameworks to identify, assess, and track the mitigation of ESG-related risks.
4	Anti-Corruption Policies	Number of anti-corruption training sessions conducted	Track the number of training sessions and participation rates among employees
5	Stakeholder Engagement	Number of stakeholder engagement meetings held.	Record the number of meetings and interactions with stakeholders regarding ESG matters.

Template for Implementing Global Reporting Initiative (GRI) on ESG Reporting

1. Introduction

Purpose of the ESG Report: Outline the objectives and goals of the ESG report.
Scope and Boundaries: Define the scope and boundaries of the report, including the reporting period.

2. Stakeholder Engagement

Identification of Stakeholders: List the key stakeholders relevant to the organization.
Engagement Process: Describe the methods and processes used for engaging with stakeholders.
Stakeholder Feedback: Summarize key feedback and how it has influenced the ESG reporting process.

3. Governance Structure

Governance Framework: Describe the governance structure of the organization.
Board Composition: Provide details on the composition and diversity of the board.
Executive Compensation: Outline how executive compensation aligns with ESG performance.
Risk Management: Describe the organization's approach to risk management, especially concerning ESG risks.
Anti-Corruption Policies: Summarize the anti-corruption policies and any incidents.

4. Materiality Assessment

Process: Explain the process used to conduct the materiality assessment.
Key ESG Issues: List the significant ESG issues identified through the assessment.

5. Data Collection and Management

Data Collection System: Describe the system and processes for collecting ESG data.
Data Verification and Validation: Outline the procedures for ensuring data accuracy and completeness.
Key Performance Indicators (KPIs): List the KPIs used to measure ESG performance.

<u>6.</u> Environmental Reporting

Greenhouse Gas Emissions: Report on direct and indirect GHG emissions.
Energy Consumption: Provide data on energy consumption and efficiency initiatives.
Water Management: Describe water usage and management practices.
Waste Management: Report on waste generation, management, and reduction efforts.
Biodiversity Impact: Outline significant impacts on biodiversity.
Environmental Compliance: Provide details on compliance and incidents of non-compliance.

<u>7.</u>Social Reporting

Diversity and Inclusion: Describe employee diversity and inclusion practices.
Labor Practices: Report on labour practices, including health and safety measures.
Employee Development: Provide data on employee training and development programs.
Community Engagement: Describe community engagement and impact initiatives.
Human Rights: Report on human rights practices and incidents.
Product Responsibility: Provide details on product responsibility, including customer health and safety.

<u>8.</u> Reporting and Communication

Report Layout: Design the report layout to ensure accessibility and clarity.
Balanced Reporting: Ensure the report provides a balanced view of ESG performance, including both positive and negative aspects.
GRI Content Index: Include a GRI Content Index to guide readers to relevant sections of the report.
External Assurance: Obtain external assurance for the ESG report, if applicable.
Stakeholder Feedback Mechanism: Set up a mechanism for responding to stakeholder feedback.

<u>9.</u> Continual Improvement

Review Process: Establish a process for regularly reviewing and updating ESG reporting practices.
Progress Tracking: Track progress against goals and objectives set in previous ESG reports.
Stakeholder Feedback Integration: Integrate stakeholder feedback into future reports.
Monitoring Changes: Continuously monitor changes in GRI Standards and other relevant guidelines.

<u>10.</u> Appendices

GRI Content Index: Detailed index mapping the report content to GRI Standards.
Glossary: Definitions of key terms and concepts used in the report.
Additional Data: Any additional data or information supporting the ESG report.

Checklist for Implementation
Global Reporting Initiative (GRI)
on ESG Reporting

General Preparation

1. [ ] Identify key stakeholders.

2. [ ] Establish an ESG reporting team.

3. [ ] Review latest GRI Standards.

4. [ ] Conduct materiality assessment.

5. [ ] Set ESG reporting goals.

6. [ ] Define report scope and boundaries.

7. [ ] Determine reporting period and frequency.

Data Collection and Management

8. [ ] Implement a data collection system.

9. [ ] Ensure consistent data collection methods.

10. [ ] Establish data verification procedures.

11. [ ] Validate reported data.

12. [ ] Utilize software tools for data management.

13. [ ] Identify KPIs for ESG aspects.

Environmental Reporting

14. [ ] Report GHG emissions.

15. [ ] Disclose energy consumption.

16. [ ] Report on water management.

17. [ ] Disclose waste management efforts.

18. [ ] Report on biodiversity impact.

19. [ ] Provide details on environmental compliance.

Social Reporting

20. [ ] Report on diversity and inclusion.

21. [ ] Disclose labour practices and health and safety measures.

22. [ ] Provide data on employee development programs.

23. [ ] Report on community engagement initiatives.

24. [ ] Disclose human rights practices.

25. [ ] Provide details on product responsibility.

Governance Reporting

26. [ ] Disclose governance structure.

27. [ ] Report on board composition.

28. [ ] Outline executive compensation alignment with ESG.

29. [ ] Disclose risk management practices.

30. [ ] Report on anti-corruption policies.

Reporting and Communication

31. [ ] Design report layout.

32. [ ] Ensure balanced reporting.

33. [ ] Include a GRI Content Index.

34. [ ] Obtain external assurance.

35. [ ] Set up stakeholder feedback mechanism.

Continuous Improvement

36. [ ] Establish a review process.

37. [ ] Track progress against goals.

38. [ ] Integrate stakeholder feedback.

39. [ ] Monitor changes in GRI Standards.